IT'S IN OUR BONES

A CONVERSATION ABOUT RACE, COURAGE AND CONNECTION

Courage, Connection and How to be a Racial Upstander

I0617177

BART BAILEY

TABLE OF CONTENTS

Letter from the Author 1

POEM: Humanity 3

FOREWORD 5

PREFACE: LEGACY 9

CHAPTER ONE: THRESHOLD 23

CHAPTER TWO: RED FLAG............................ 41

CHAPTER THREE: THE WRINKLED SHIRT...................... 49

CHAPTER FOUR: DEBT OWED 55

CHAPTER FIVE: YES, HOPE CAN WORK 73

CHAPTER SIX: THE INVISIBLE HEROES........................ 79

CHAPTER SEVEN: THE THIN BLACK AND BLUE LINE 95

CHAPTER EIGHT: STAY WOKE 113

CHAPTER NINE: MY DAD, THE BOND, AND THE MYTH OF SCARCITY..121

CHAPTER TEN: MENTAL WEALTH 129

CHAPTER ELEVEN: THE KAEPERNICK FACTOR............ 137

CHAPTER TWELVE: THE BLACK BOARDROOM............ 147

CHAPTER THIRTEEN: THE LURE 151

CHAPTER FOURTEEN: THIRTY WAYS TO IMPROVE RACE RELATIONS 157

EPILOGUE: TRUTH AND RECONCILIATION............... 167

ACKNOWLEDGMENTS 180

ABOUT THE AUTHOR.. 183

All rights reserved. No part of this publication or its characters may be reproduced, distributed, or transmitted in any form or by any means, including photocopying, recording, or other electronic or mechanical methods, without the prior written permission of the publisher, except in the case of brief quotations embodied in reviews and certain other noncommercial uses permitted by copyright law.

Library of Congress Cataloging-in-Publication Data is available upon request.

©2025 Copyright Bart Bailey. All Rights Reserved

Printed in the United States of America

LETTER FROM THE AUTHOR

Dear Readers,

This book is about the layers of our identity that shape our beliefs and decision-making. It is an invitation to honor those conscious and unconscious learnings that become baked into our bones over time. My hope is that by sharing some of the things that shape who I am, you will feel inspired to reflect on the things that shape who you are.

I am learning to let go of those things that hinder my ability to connect with others. One of my definitions of growth involves learning to allow fear, anxiety, and even the physical body to become a teacher. It is through welcoming all of these experiences that we can begin to address racism, bias, and the dynamics of othering.

I strive to be a good ancestor in this moment, knowing that it is a lifelong journey. This book is written for anyone who is willing to walk alongside me on this path. I love the beautiful imperfection of humans who are committed to working on their connections with others, embracing both personal and societal flaws.

As you engage with this book, I encourage you to keep a journal with you. Let it serve as a space to witness your own story unfolding alongside mine. Together, may we grow and deepen our understanding of ourselves and each other.

With gratitude,

Bart Bailey

Humanity

Diane H. Dalzell

We are humans to our very core
Bumbling through the hurdles that knock on our door
We breathe through the veins of our ancestors
And struggle with the pain that festers
We carry the weight from our past on our shoulders
Like the flow of hot lava smolders
Generations have struggled to break the curse
While rhetoric repeats its ugly verse
We have the capacity to be intelligent
To speak a tongue and be in our own element
To be creative and make judgement
To be conscious and to live benevolent
To see through my skin; and love me for me

To possess the empathy for my neighbor; or my enemy

To shine with the God given resilience

Despite the destruction and pestilence

To lean in when we err

And pay homage to what is fair

To protect our minds, bodies and souls

From the age old stories we've been told

To seek out the dignity of hope

To allow for grace and; an inch of rope

To share in the equality of our truths

And have the audacity to listen in our disputes

To forge ahead with a newfound spirit

To look inward and have patience to hear it

To see your pain as my own

And advocate together on our throne

It's the lessons learned from our father and our mother

Its realizing... I am your brother

It's the ability to do the work undone

And honor the past, the present and the future as one!

FOREWORD

In *It's in our Bones: A Conversation About Race, Courage and Connection*, Bart Bailey does an extraordinary job of weaving the personal and historical to provide an illuminating introduction to the important work he does to foster conversations about race. As the senior vice dean for faculty for Drexel University College of Medicine and the executive director of Executive Leadership in Academic Medicine® (ELAM), the nation's only longitudinal leadership program for women in academic medicine, dentistry, public health and pharmacy, and our new program, Executive Leadership in Health Care (ELH) for women executives in hospitals and health care systems, I have been fortunate to incorporate Mr. Bailey's work into our curriculum. He has made a tremendous impact on the ELAM and ELH fellowships and on the leadership of the programs. He has helped us delve into the deep veins of racism that stretch throughout the field of medicine and recognize both our individual and collective responsibility to demand, create and support anti-racist policies and practices in our institutions. Racism in medicine has led to unequal access to healthcare services, resulting in poorer outcomes for certain racial and ethnic groups; bias in treatment; stereotyping in diagnosis; and overall lack of representation in the field. Mr. Bailey has helped us to create a learning environment that enables frank, open and honest conversations around race and race and medicine.

I hope you take your time to read this book deeply and with curiosity. I urge you to take the opportunity to immerse yourself in the process of journaling as you read and grow through each chapter.

Mr. Bailey's goal of recognizing the humanity and worthiness in all of us is one we should all be striving for. As Mr. Bailey asks us in the book, "What is your legacy?"

Nancy D. Spector, MD
Professor of Pediatrics
Betty A. Cohen Chair in Women's Health
Senior Vice Dean for Faculty
Executive Director, Lynn Yeakel Institute for Women's

Health and Leadership (IWHL)
Executive Director, Executive Leadership in Academic Medicine® (ELAM) and Executive Leadership in Health Care
Drexel University College of Medicine

LEGACY

My mother, like so many Black women before her, and like so many since, is a hero. To understand me, the mission of this book, and as we learn to talk to one another—just talk, the simplest of things—while navigating the thorniness that is race in America, you must understand Dorothy Bailey.

There's a core belief she has: "Service is the purpose of being alive." This may sound quaint in today's frenetic world where our short attention spans and hurried lives don't always allow time for us to slow down and recognize the contributions of others, but the saying fits her perfectly.

Dorothy's life of dedication to others is impossible to miss. Neither my bias, as her son, nor my pride of her success can delineate her influence as a dedicated civil rights activist and politician. Her leadership stretched across portions of the Eastern Seaboard, from North Carolina to Maryland to Pennsylvania. The effect of her work was felt by hundreds, if not thousands, of people. She is exuberant, kind, and introspective. She is scholarly and fearless (unless it came to driving at night in the rain). She has spent her life taking on every challenge and like so many Black women who bear the dual burden of raising a family and protecting them from a world that sometimes doesn't treat people of color with respect, or worse, the stress of fighting forced her to seek solace when things closed in too fast.

Even one of her sanctuaries showed the kind of person she is. Often, she took refuge in one of Prince George's County library rooms that housed collections from Black activists, including Sojourner Truth and Mary McLeod Bethune, among others.

"You had in that room all kinds of historical documents," she once said. "I would go in there and get lost, and especially when my children got on my nerves [that would be me, Bart]. My husband got on my last, good nerve, and after I became an elected official, when it got hot on the council, that was my place of refuge. I'd lock the door and pretend you didn't hear anyone else trying to get into that room. I could feel Sojourner and all of those people, and Mary McLeod Bethune, just rinsing all over my body, and when I would leave, I'd feel so much better. I was then again ready to go out and greet the world."

My mom is an explorer, except instead solely for financial gain, she has sought life experiences. The lessons she learned were passed down to me, and my sister, Robbin, and there were many lessons because Dorothy did so much. She served on Prince George's County Council for almost a decade, twice serving as its chairperson. She established a Harlem Renaissance Festival in the county which started in 1999. Here's what *The Washington Post* once wrote: "Dorothy Bailey, chairwoman of the Harlem Remembrance Foundation, and Prince George's County Council member Andrea C. Harrison (D) opened the festival. Bailey said it was 'an opportunity to showcase some of the talent that we have in Prince George's County...We have to pass it down' or 'it will die'" (*The Washington Post*, 1999).

Dorothy was on the boards of the National Council of Negro Women, started in 1935 by Bethune, which is an organization dedicated to bettering the lives of Black women; and the Association for the Study of African American Life and History, which was founded in Chicago in 1915. In 2014, after decades of service across the state,

Dorothy was inducted into the Maryland Women's Hall of Fame, joining such remarkable people as Odessa M. Shannon (recipient of the Lifetime Achievement Award for volunteerism awarded by President Barack Obama), Nancy K. Welker (physicist and expert in superconductors), Dominique Dawes (Olympic gymnast), and Sandra Williams Ortega (the first Black woman from Maryland commissioned as an Air Force officer), among others (Maryland Women's Hall of Fame, 2014).

Dorothy even wrote a book. In 2011, she published *In A Different Light: Reflections and Beauty of Wise Women of Color*. She interviewed 90 influential Maryland women aged 70 or older, including one who was 100. The book's foreword was written by Dr. Julianne Malveaux, an author and economist with a doctorate in economics from Massachusetts Institute of Technology (MIT). She was also a syndicated columnist for *USA Today* and a regular contributor to CNN and Black Entertainment Television (BET). Malveaux began the foreword with a Senegalese proverb: "When an old person dies, a library burns to the ground" (Malveaux, 2011).

In an exquisite moment of game-recognizes-game, Malveaux added: "I am reminded of the Senegalese proverb when I flip through the rich pages of *In A Different Light* that was clearly lovingly compiled by Dorothy Bailey, a woman of accomplishment and a font of wisdom in her own right. In lifting up the stories of some of Maryland's wise women of color, Bailey not only preserves libraries that might otherwise burn, but also asserts the need for women of color to impart their wisdom, be it mother-wit, philosophical musing, or scholarly knowledge, just as others do" (Malveaux, 2011).

In the book, my mom called these great women "wisdom carriers." She, herself, is one of those people.

She attended North Carolina Central University, one of the schools that staged sit-ins across the state. These sit-ins were brave acts of non-violence and one of the sparks of the civil rights movement. The Greensboro Four—four students from the University of North Carolina who sat down on Feb. 1, 1960, at the lunch counter of a segregated Woolworth's and refused to leave when asked—are among the highest profile examples. That moment, and the idea of it as a nonviolent sit-in serving as a tool to fight Jim Crow, spread across Black schools in the South and was pivotal in bringing attention to the ugliness of segregation. Eventually Woolworth's, and other businesses, were forbidden from denying service to Black Americans.

My mom joined the civil rights protests in the state and once, while marching, an egg hit her in the back of the head. "When something hits you in the back of the neck," she once said about that moment, "you don't know if that soft, light stuff is blood...you don't know whether you've been shot...so you're terrified. [But] one of the things Dr. King and our leaders said was, 'Never stop. Don't talk to anybody. Just walk straight ahead and just keep moving, keep moving. And I remember to this very day, 'I just gotta' keep moving.'"

Just keep moving. It's advice we can all follow, no matter our political beliefs. Just keep going.

Why am I telling you all of this about Dorothy? Why should you care? Her full life isn't just an example for me. Her belief system, her ideals, are ones we can all absorb. Dorothy believes we are each here, on Earth, to complete a particular assignment. It is her way of saying we are here to create legacies. That's what we do. In our personal lives, our work ones, with our friends...they remember us and what we have done for them or, sometimes even, what we failed to do.

Our legacy isn't necessarily about the degrees you earn. As my mom would say, degrees will be in your obituary. What fulfills you, what makes you you, what pushes you... those are the building blocks of a legacy.

My life, my belief, down to my bones, is to create a world where we all live together free of hate. However, I am also unapologetically Black, and you will see that here as well. Pro-Black isn't anti-white. Pro-Black isn't anti-anything. I'm reminded of a book called, *Why Black People Tend to Shout* from the late Ralph Wiley. "Why do Black people tend to shout...? When a sweet grandmotherly sort has to tell you how Black people once were chained in iron masks in the canebrake, to keep them from eating the cane while they harvested it, and that these masks were like little ovens that cooked the skin off their faces—when you hear that grandmotherly voice and realize she once was a girl who might have been your girl, and someone caused this pain on her lips and nobody did anything about it but keep living –this gives you a tendency to shout..."

The goal of this book is to introduce you to me and my work, which is fostering conversations about race, and bridging divides. I also want to use this work as a history lesson, speaking about legendary Black heroes, particularly the forgotten ones.

Mainly, I just want to talk to you. Black people have talked bluntly about race for generations. Because we must. For other races, however, there have been 400 years of not practicing these conversations.

What's clear by now is we must work through our differences because there is no going back to the past. There are swaths of the American people who do want to travel back in time, back to the 1950s, when Black people didn't have the right to vote, and people of color overall were seen as less than.

This kind of nostalgia figured extensively in the 2016 presidential campaign between Hillary Clinton and the man I will never name. (I won't mention him because he represents everything I oppose.) Robert Jones wrote in his book *The End of White Christian America:* "The election, more than in any in recent memory, came down to two vividly contrasting views of America. [The former President's] campaign painted a bleak portrait of America's present, set against a bright, if monochromatic, vision of 1950s America restored. Hillary Clinton's campaign, by contrast, sought to replace the first African American president with the first female president and embraced the multicultural future of 2050, the year the Census Bureau originally projected the United States would become a majority nonwhite nation. 'Make America Great Again' and 'Stronger Together,' the two campaigns' competing slogans, became proxies for an epic battle over the changing face of America."

This isn't a new notion. Far from it. James Baldwin, one of the greatest writers of the 20th century, addressed the notion of whites wanting to turn back the clock. On April 28, 1986, about eight months before his death, Baldwin spoke at the Coolidge Auditorium at the Library of Congress in Washington, D.C., and he read from his book *Notes of a Native Son*, starting purposely with the part of his work that dealt with fear of a Black planet.

"Yet, if the American Negro has arrived at his identity by virtue of the absoluteness of his estrangement from his past, American white men still nourish the illusion that there is some means of recovering the European innocence, of returning to a state in which black men do not exist," Baldwin wrote. "This is one of the greatest errors Americans can make. The identity they fought so hard to protect has, by virtue of that battle, undergone a change: Americans are as unlike any other white people in the world as it is possible to be. I do not think, for example, that it is too much to suggest that the American vision of the world—which allows so little reality, generally speaking, for any of the darker forces in human life, which tends until today to paint moral issues in glaring black and white—owes a great deal to the battle waged by Americans to maintain between themselves and black men a human separation which could not be bridged. It is only now beginning to be borne in on us, very faintly, it must be admitted, very slowly, and very much against our will—that this vision of the world is dangerously inaccurate, and perfectly useless. For it protects our moral high-mindedness at the terrible expense of weakening our grasp of reality. People who shut their eyes to reality simply invite their own destruction, and anyone who insists on remaining in a state of innocence long after that innocence is dead turns himself into a monster."

No, this isn't a new notion, but it's still highly relevant now, and in many ways, we are at one of the more critical moments in this country's history. "Ever since it became clear to me that what we are dealing with is a confederate insurgency, I've wondered how all this will end," wrote journalist Nancy LeTourneau in the *Washington Monthly*. "Obviously I'm terrible at predictions, so it's not worth it to try. All I know is that the last two times this country faced a challenge like this (the Civil War and the civil rights movement), too much blood was spilled...In other words, no matter how hard [the former President's supporters] try, the 1950's aren't coming back, and many of us don't want them to. We either face the future together, or eventually, all hell breaks loose."

What I know, what I've lived, and what I've seen is that people can work together. When we put aside our biases, we certainly can. In May of 2021, for example, I had a gathering of neighbors in front of my home in Pennsylvania. I asked a few dozen of my neighbors a question: what does it mean to live in a beloved community? I compiled some of their responses below:

"A Beloved Community is one that is filled with LOVE and CARE for one another;"

"A Beloved Community is one that offers a sense of BELONGING and SUPPORT;"

"A Beloved Community is one that exhibits FRIENDLINESS and RESPECT for all;"

"A Beloved Community exudes a feeling of TOGETHERNESS. There is HELP during times of hardship and support to alleviate one another;"

"A Beloved Community is one that is SAFE with the help of everyone;"

"A Beloved Community fosters an environment that is INCLUSIVE;"

"A Beloved Community is one that is EQUITABLE;"

"A Beloved Community is one that feels like a FAMILY."

The connective tissue of all the responses is togetherness. My neighbors are a mix of all kinds of people, from different backgrounds, and have made the choice to do the work.

In 2008, a writer for *Forbes* declared after the election of President Barack Obama: "So, in answer to the question, 'Is America past racism against Black people,' I say the answer is yes." Of course, 12 years later, George Floyd was murdered. Declaring the end of racism is *not* doing the work. This is a long journey and claims of not seeing color or an end to racism is false. There's no such thing as the end of racism or being color blind.

I tell people to be color brave and not color blind. What does that mean? It means talking about race in a compassionate, informed, and fearless way isn't just important; it's required. It means talking about race is an act of bravery and can help avoid potentially embarrassing, or worse situations. I remember a story that comes from finance executive Mellody Hobson during a TED Talk she gave in 2014. She tells the remarkable—but unsurprising to most of Black America—moment when a Black candidate for U.S. Senate in Tennessee, Harold Ford, was looking to energize his campaign. One of Hobson's media contacts suggested a meeting with that newspaper's editorial board and when she and Ford arrived at the building, both Black, both dressed professionally, the desk receptionist took them to a back room and then asked: "Where are your uniforms?" The receptionist thought the two— one a Senate candidate, and the other a highly connected and brilliant financier, who in 2020, would become the chairwoman of Starbucks Corporation, making her the first Black woman to become chairwoman of an S&P 500 company—were the kitchen help.

"Now, race is one of those topics in America that

makes people extraordinarily uncomfortable," Hobson said. "You bring it up at a dinner party or in a workplace environment, it is literally the conversational equivalent of touching the third rail. There is shock, followed by a long silence. And even coming here today, I told some friends and colleagues that I planned to talk about race, and they warned me, they told me, 'Don't do it,' that there'd be huge risks in me talking about this topic, that people might think I'm a militant Black woman and I would ruin my career. And I must tell you, I actually for a moment was a bit afraid. Then I realized, the first step to solving any problem is to not hide from it, and the first step to any form of action is awareness. And so I decided to actually talk about race. And I decided that if I came here and shared with you some of my experiences, that maybe we could all be a little less anxious and a little more bold in our conversations about race."

In other words, when it comes to race, be smart, be kind, *be brave.*

This book will deal with issues of race because the times we're in require that, and throughout it will note that we all come from different places. As my mom says, what's in our cores is our upbringing. It impacts us in many ways, and while it doesn't define us, it shapes how we view the world, particularly when it comes to how we view those who look different from us.

I want to make it clear that this book will not blame, shame, or guilt people to be different. This book is about honesty, ownership, and accountability around truth telling and dealing with harm that hinders our humanity.

I'm going to ask uncomfortable questions, chances are they will make you think or squirm or reflect—or some version of all those things. I believe our growth is in the sweet spot of discomfort and curiosity. I'm emotionally exoskeletal—meaning, I can be blunt, because I believe talking about race requires bluntness.

The most central question this book will invite you to is a question my mom would often ask: What is your legacy?

CHAPTER ONE

THRESHOLD

During the birth of my son, Ivan, my wife was at a well-known New York hospital. As the delivery progressed, the medical staff decided she should be given an epidural. But there was a problem. As one of the doctors started, it was clear the epidural was causing extreme pain. It was not discomfort. It was pain. The epidural was the problem, not her contraction. Her pain, however, was being ignored despite her saying how much it hurt.

I was in the room, close to her, and it got so bad, and the doctor was so uncaring about her pain, that I had to step in and tell them to stop. The epidural was stopped, and the pain decreased.

In that moment, and later when thinking about what happened, I wondered how many Black women in that hospital, and other hospitals—not just now but across many different hospitals, across many decades, even centuries—were forced to endure terrible pain because it was just expected for Black women to do so.

None of this is to say that all doctors are this way. There are plenty who are caring and empathetic. This was my experience and not the experience of everyone, and, again, many doctors, including ones that I'm close with, exhibit great care and meticulousness.

Ivan was born, and about three days later he had open-heart surgery. He had a condition called Tetralogy of Fallot. It's an extremely rare condition caused by heart defects at birth (Centers for Disease Control and Prevention, 2022). If doctors were oblivious, if not racially insensitive, during the attempted epidural, the nursing staff was the opposite. They were empathetic and caring. Mainly, they helped me get over my fear that my son could die. It was a rare situation for me because I wasn't in control. I couldn't just take my son home. I had to see him get operated on, and it was scary.

We were in the hospital for three consecutive months. One of us was always with Ivan. We rotated shifts and passed a notebook back and forth with notes about our observations of him. I was afraid of holding Ivan initially because he was so small, and I didn't want to hurt him. Then, a nurse had a come-to-Jesus moment with me, and she forced Ivan into my arms. It was one of those beautiful moments a parent never forgets and, in some ways, marked the beginning of the relationship with my incredible son.

That nurse bathed Ivan like he was any other child. She scrubbed that little body and washed his hair. She lovingly roughed him up. The nursing staff helped me see him beyond his condition—he was just my son. I loved the care they extended to him. During those three months, we became like family. In fact, one day there was a severe storm, and I drove to pick up a nurse to come into work so the nurse on shift could go home and sleep.

In the end, Ivan was normal and healthy, and overall, our experience at that hospital was a good one. Yet that moment with the epidural and the pain my wife experienced, and how it was ignored, reminded me of something: history. Particularly the history of race and medicine in America.

Human beings don't always learn from history. There's a saying that originated with Mark Twain. He said, "History never repeats itself, but it does rhyme" (Twain, 1885). There isn't a better example of the rhyme than how the medical profession treats Black people.

Our pain isn't seen as real pain. It's ignored. We're viewed as physically superhuman, able to withstand discomfort more than other races (Hoffman et al., 2016). It's not accidental. Like so many other things about race, it is old and historic and deeply rooted.

Racism is a monster, like ski-masked Jason in *Friday the 13th*, and it will not die unless you consistently attack it. In America, we continuously fail at realizing this. In some cases, purposefully so. In others, accidentally so. There are segments of politics and the media who traffic in extremism and hate and are more than happy to forget history.

What do I mean by the history of Black pain, and how doctors have traditionally treated us as less than human? This is a needed conversation, as important as any other when it comes to race, because there is nothing more central to the humanity of all people than our medical needs, and how we are treated when we are suffering.

—

You cannot talk about race in America without discussing how Black people are still viewed by a significant swath of doctors and others in the dominant culture here in the United States as animalistic. This view goes back centuries and is still prevalent now. It's rooted in slavery.

Some people, especially some white people, when you talk about the impact of slavery, their eyes roll. There is a belief among a certain group of Americans that slavery was so long ago, and it has no impact on the modern world. In some cases, they are simply ignorant about history. In others, they want to act like slavery never existed, or it wasn't so bad, or that its awful impact stopped being felt decades or even centuries ago.

Let's go back in time to the early days of the establishment of the colonies in America and the eventual introduction of slavery. Remarkably, in the early stages of the nation's development, as Nikole Hannah-Jones' *1619 Project* notes, there was no classification for race (Hannah-Jones, 2019). Race wasn't established until slavery, and that was because, to be blunt, slave owners began raping enslaved women with impunity. It was legal to do so because Black women were property.

In many cases, these barbaric acts would result in children, and the children were biracial. Slave owners weren't certain what to do with these Black and white children. After all, they weren't going to let them be citizens. They couldn't. They were part Black.

British law, which was patrilineal, dictated that the children should have had the status of their fathers. Those fathers were white. But if these kids had that status, they could have ended the horrific financial enterprise that was slavery, since they would have been entitled to their father's wealth (Higginbotham, 1978).

Slave owners needed a classification system to prevent that, and they invented one. This is how official racial classification was born in America. In Virginia, in 1662, the General Assembly of Virginia passed a law that stated Black women would have the status of their mothers. In other words, not only did these children have no rights, but they were also officially enslaved. The law read: "Negro women's children to serve according to the condition of their mother" (*Statutes at Large of Virginia*, 1662).

When I talk about how race is an artificial construct, this is one of many examples of what I mean. Slave owners created an instant political classification and made the source of that classification a Black woman's womb. They attempted to make it seem as if slavery was an inherited condition. Not only that. It was a way for slave owners to blame Black women for the enslaved status of their children.

To justify the barbarism of slavery, white people created an entire culture—and by extension an entire economy—on the belief that people from Africa were an inferior race. By the 1800s, a genre of junk (pseudoscience) science would emerge attempting to justify that belief. White religious leaders used the Bible and God to do the same. Much of the media at the time also parroted these themes.

In 1851, a pro-slavery scientific leader of the time, Dr. Samuel Cartwright, presented a report to the Louisiana Medical Association called "The Diseases and Peculiarities of the Negro Race." One of its many absurd statements was the invention of a new disease called "Drapetomania." Cartwright had stated Black people were different physiologically from white people, possessing smaller brains. The traits, unique to Black people, gave Black people an especially high propensity for servitude (Cartwright, 1851). Cartwright also said, "the Negro slave is a slave by nature and can never be happy...in any other condition."

Cartwright was far from alone with his scientific racism. This type of pseudoscience popped up almost everywhere, and the core of it was utilized to justify slavery. Medical journals contained entries about Black people having smaller skulls and thicker skin (Savitt, 2007).

It is in this period, also, where you began to see constant references to Black people having higher pain thresholds. In fact, it would become a commonality among the so-called scientific community, particularly in the Southern slave states. This is where the fallacy of the ability of Black people to have superhuman ability to endure pain was born—in the pro-slavery era of our country.

What happened to my wife in that hospital room can be traced back to ideas like this. The notion that Black bodies' pain tolerance is exceptional is directly linked to the enslavement of Black bodies.

Perhaps the vilest part of this era (and there are many from which to pick) were the experiments done on Black people, particularly Black women. Physicians and others used the fake science that stated Black people were essentially animals to justify a level of experimental grotesquery rarely seen in the nation at that time.

Black women bore the brunt of this. During the 1800s, J. Marion Sims, the father of modern gynecology, conducted medical experiments to advance the field exclusively on enslaved women. He operated on them without anesthesia—despite it being available—based on the racist belief that Black women were immune to pain (Owens, 2017).

While so much of this horrific history has been under-taught or even erased, what Sims did, as part of the country's racial reckoning after the murder of George Floyd, came more to light. It wasn't just social justice issues that were reexamined after Floyd's killing; it was reexamining the bloody legacies of men like Sims. Do we have the capacity for truth telling and the ability to honor the proper legacy?

Centuries later, what's become clear is the falsity of Black women's ability to not feel pain still impacts the reproductive healthcare they get. One 2016 study showed that Black patients get undertreated for pain relative to white patients, partly because some healthcare providers believe that Black and white people are biologically different (Hoffman et al., 2016).

Overall, the medical field is failing Black women. The maternal mortality rate of Black women is more than double that of white women. The reason has nothing to do with actual biology (CDC, 2021).

The results of a groundbreaking new study published in 2023 that examined two million births in California were indicative of this issue. The study found that the richest Black mothers and their babies are twice as likely to die as the richest white mothers and theirs. As *The New York Times* notes, the study was unique in that it combined income tax data with birth, death, and hospitalization records, along with demographic data from the Census Bureau and the Social Security Administration (Rossin-Slater et al., 2023).

The study showed something predictable but still maddening. The infants born to the wealthiest families were less likely to die than the ones born to poor parents. Yet, as the *Times* writes, one group didn't receive the same protection from being wealthy: Black mothers and babies.

"It suggests that the well-documented Black-white gap in infant and maternal health that's been discussed a lot in recent years is not just explained by differences in economic circumstances," Maya Rossin-Slater, an economist studying health policy at Stanford and an author of the study, told the *Times*. "It suggests it's much more structural" (Rossin-Slater et al., 2023).

There's other data to support this. A survey done by BioMed Central found that almost 23 percent of Black women were mistreated by medical staff. That mistreatment included violations of physical privacy, being threatened, or refused treatment. That number compares to just 14.1 percent of white women (Vedam et al., 2019). The survey included this interesting finding: "Regardless of maternal race, having a partner who was Black also increased reported mistreatment." In other words, Black women can be mistreated not only because they are Black women, but also because their partner is Black.

"This is the first study to use indicators developed by service users to describe mistreatment in childbirth in the U.S.," the study writes in its conclusion. "Our findings suggest that mistreatment is experienced more frequently by women of (color), when birth occurs in hospitals, and among those with social, economic or health challenges..."

So much of this information about the health disparities between Black Americans and other races was covered expertly by the *New York Times' 1619 Project*. One of the writers for the project—and the main impetus behind its reporting on the health disparities—is an author named Linda Villarosa. Like others, she once believed the gap was due to poverty, but that view would change. She came to think the problem was due to "weathering," a newer perspective that suggests societal racism takes a heavy medical toll on Black people by creating wear and tear on the body. It's a concept developed by Dr. Arlene Geronimus, a public health professor.

"Your heart rate goes up; your cortisol stress levels go up in your body. Your blood pressure rises," she said in a 2023 interview with NPR. "It's not good for the body. But when people are treated badly, that's what happens."

Villarosa added that one of the key other issues remains the view that Black people can endure more pain than other races. In 2019, she told NPR that a study by researchers from UNC-Chapel Hill showed Black women failed to receive the same level of pain management following a C-section as white women.

It didn't matter that all the conditions were the same. Villarosa said a possible explanation is the implicit biases of medical students and residents.

"That is alarming...," she said, "and so that means that we need to do things differently here."

"We're not accusing individuals of being racist, but we're saying there is something wrong with what is happening in America," she explained. "When you identify the problem, when you discuss the problem, it's easier to address the problem and come up with solutions than it is when you're pretending like it doesn't exist."

These disparate treatments are so prevalent across so many planks of the medical profession that it is difficult to keep track of them all. In another example, the *New York Times* reported that Black pregnant women are tested more frequently for drug use than their white counterparts. Researchers explained that racial bias was the only explanation for the difference. Black women, in fact, the study says, were less likely than white women to test positive for drug use.

Racial bias even shows up in something that would seem as non-racial as a kidney transplant. Studies have shown that Black patients have had to wait longer for kidney transplants than other races partly because of an outdated, and somewhat racist, test that once overestimated kidney function in Black patients. This resulted in longer wait times for Black kidney transplant hopefuls. In 2014, the average wait time for Black patients was 64 months, and the wait time for white patients was about half of that.

Recently, the organization that runs the nation's transplant system banned the test and instructed every transplant program to credit Black patients with time. It's a good correction. It's restorative justice, but think of all the Black patients who died waiting for a kidney as white patients passed them by–lost solely because of the color of their skin.

—

How does all of this relate to that moment, where my wife was in pain, and that pain was ignored? How does it relate to why you're reading this book? The connection is history. The data shows parts of the medical profession still hold the attitude that Black people are biologically different. That leads to the belief that we can take massive amounts of pain because we're more like animals than human beings.

My main goal is to encourage everyone to see each other as human and worthy. It's a simple goal but think about it in your own life. Do you always practice this belief?

There are four basic truisms about race and the healthcare system that need to be addressed, according to medical professionals and researchers who study this issue:

1. Racism can lead to unequal access to healthcare services, which can result in differences in health outcomes between racial and ethnic groups.

2. Racism can lead to bias and discrimination in medical treatment, where some patients are

treated differently based on their race, resulting in disparities in health outcomes.

3. Stereotyping and assumption-based diagnoses are still a problem. Health care providers may hold unconscious biases or racial stereotypes that influence their diagnostic decisions, which can result in misdiagnosis or suboptimal treatment.

4. Lack of diversity in the medical field can lead to perpetuating racism in medicine, as patients from minority groups may not have access to providers who understand their unique cultural and social backgrounds.

———

One of the things we need to do, we need to always do, is tell the truth about our history. Remembering our history, even the ugly parts, even the atrocities, helps us prevent future ones. I want you to remember a piece of data. In 1790, according to the first U.S. Census ever taken, there were approximately 700,000 enslaved people. That number skyrocketed to almost four million by 1860.

Why the explosion in the number of slaves? In 1808, Congress banned the importation of Africans into the country. That meant slave owners had to improvise since their supply of human beings was cut off. So, they turned the wombs of Black women into conveyor belts, the way auto manufacturers churn out cars This was the reality and utterly disgusting. We should tell the truth and never forget it.

We should also never forget that what grew from that bloody enterprise, particularly the use of enslaved women and their babies as profit, still has its tentacles in today's societal and medical world in more ways than one.

The rape of Black women by white men was so prevalent that it changed the genome of Black people in America. According to the American Journal of Human Genetics, 25 percent of Black people in America can be traced back to Europe through the paternal part of the family.

Since enslaved women were forced to work right up until delivery in horrible and unsanitary conditions, it's believed that there may have been hundreds of thousands, and possibly millions, of stillborn children throughout the centuries of slavery in America. Black women were often forced to give birth to as many as ten to twelve children but only half would survive.

Today, the infant mortality rate for Black babies is still staggering. Black women suffer the highest infant mortality rates in the industrialized world. In effect, Black women still carry the trauma of slavery with them. According to the American Medical Association, in the United States,

Black women are two to six times more likely to die from complications of pregnancy than white women. It's a public health crisis that remains practically uninvestigated.

It also doesn't matter how wealthy a Black mother is. Black women from all parts of the economic spectrum die. One of the highest profile cases was tennis superstar Serena Williams, one of the richest athletes in the world, who almost died after giving birth.

So much must change but despite the dangers and horrors, I remain optimistic. Why? I gave a seminar to a group of nurses in 2022, and we talked openly and honestly about bias. It was four dozen nurses from across the country and with different backgrounds. Their willingness to truly be authentic and genuine gave me hope. In truth the nurses talked about reimagining nursing and engaging with the whole person. Nurses on the receiving end of micro and macro aggressions finding their voice. Find their voice in a way to invite the offender into their lived experience. Allies moving from bystanders to upstanders and willing to challenge cultural and historical norms for the rights of people being oppressed.

In many ways, what I saw with the nurses on an almost organic level was them utilize the Nonviolent Communication model developed by Marshall Rosenberg. The model invites you to explore what you observed, your feelings about your observation, your needs in this moment and what is your request. He created it in the 1960s as a way of fighting bigotry. He wanted people to connect with their own humanness and that of others. He taught NVC around the world for over 50 years.

The two overarching themes for NVC are empathy and honesty, and the nurses displayed that in bunches. The nurses of color spoke bluntly about the challenges they face in the profession, and the white nurses and how they learned to understand their own weak spots when engaging with all patients. These conversations are only a start, but a start is needed. From there, comes progress.

And when progress is made, Black women like my wife will be treated with the empathy and care they deserve.

—

The reason Black people continue to examine the medical profession, giving it the much-needed dissection it deserves, is to protect the lives of Black women and Black babies. There's also something else. We deserve the same opportunities to build families made of love and care in the same way that white families do. Our family was given the opportunity to do that and Ivan's brother, Kalil, who is 10 years older, is our other love. Kalil has known what it's been like to be loved and cared for by two attentive parents. He also remembers his little brother being born, and he jumped right into that older brother protective mode.

Kalil understood that his mom was pregnant, and his little brother had a condition that was identified prior to birth. Kalil was concerned for his little brother, but he also had a question after Ivan came into the world: "Am I still going to get some loving?"

We understood why he asked that question, and we assured him: "Yes, son we got you!"

Kalil called Ivan his hero; he knew his little brother was fighting, and Ivan loves his brother. That is another reason to put the medical profession under a racial microscope—Black families want the same chance to exist, to live, to prosper.

THE FINAL WORD: One thing I'll emphasize in this book is for you to journal your own thoughts. It's important because I don't want this to be a one-way experience. I want you to join me and bring your own life experiences into this journey. In reading this chapter, please consider something important: how does the hospital and medical system treat *all* people? Keep in mind there are plenty of excellent doctors and nurses, but they work within a system that isn't always equitable or fair to people of color.

CHAPTER TWO:

RED FLAG

A few years ago, we went to a campsite in Virginia. My sister and brother-in-law had been going there for quite some time. In fact, his family has been going there for generations. When we arrived at the site there was a group of guys playing horseshoes. One guy had the Confederate flag emblem on both his hat and tank top.

If you don't understand why the Confederate flag is so offensive—to many people but especially to Black people— let me explain it. The primary reason the Confederacy existed was to keep slavery—the central economic engine of the South—intact, and thus, maintain one of the cruelest and most horrendous acts in this country's history (McPherson, 1990). If you wear that flag, you are making a statement, especially to Black people, and that statement is that you don't care about the pain and suffering of Black human beings. You are, essentially, mocking that pain.

What many backers of the flag say is it's about honoring the heritage of the South.

"In a 2019 survey of nearly 35,000 U.S. adults, polling firm YouGov found that although a plurality of Americans (41 percent) thinks the flag symbolizes racism, 34 percent think it symbolizes heritage," wrote *National Geographic* in 2021. "In the wake of the 2017 Charlottesville white supremacist rally, demand for the banner surged across the country" (Vora, 2021).

National Geographic added:

"By the early 20th century, white Southerners had mythologized an imagined South that fought the war not to uphold slavery but to protect states' rights and a genteel way of life—an idyll endangered by 'Northern aggression' and interference. As historian Caroline E. Janney notes, the Lost Cause myth came about immediately after the war as Confederates struggled to come to terms with their defeat 'in a postwar climate of economic, racial, and social uncertainty'" (Janney, 2016).

The heritage argument has always been a lie. Many of the people who support the flag, and say they do so because of heritage, don't even have families from the South. It remains, at its core, a symbol of hate (Coski, 2005).

So, all of this was in play when I saw the man wearing that flag. I know all this history, and it was clear when we spoke that he did not. And yes, we spoke.

The flags weren't just present on the clothing of individuals, we saw large flags flying over some lots as well. I jokingly asked my sister: "What have you gotten us into?" My sister said, "They do their thing, we do our thing, it's been going on for years, just come on in."

We continued, parked the car, saw my family, and had a good time. Later in the day, we were standing in line for a ride in a horse drawn carriage and the same man wearing the Confederate flag hat and shirt was in line with us, with his three grandchildren in tow. I had thought there would be separate carriages for his family and mine but there weren't. We ended up on the same carriage together.

Now, I'm fuming because I have to sit in the same carriage as this guy with the flag. I finally couldn't take it any longer.

"Dude," I said, "let's talk about those colors you got on."

He said: "Huh?"

I asked him to explain what those colors meant to

him, and he responded—as many backers of using the Confederate flag do—that it was about heritage. Like so many of those people, he wasn't from the South. Thus, it wasn't about heritage. However, I listened with deep curiosity. I wanted him to give me something that would link to understanding.

I then told him what that flag means to me. I said it's racist, tied to oppression, tied to white supremacy, tied to people being enslaved. Then he told me how he loves all people, and he has a Black friend. Yes, he said he has a Black friend.

The ride ended, we got out of the carriage, and the man's son approached me and apologized to us (I think one of the grandchildren told the son about our conversation). Later in the day, the man came over to our site, with Jell-O shots, and he had changed his clothes. We spoke for about an hour, and one of the things he made sure we knew was that he'd removed the Confederate flag from his trailer.

We had a great conversation, and there's a simple lesson here. I engaged with him out of curiosity. Which opened the space for me to share with him. I don't believe his beliefs had been challenged in this manner, in a way that held his dignity. Or had not been challenged by someone who knew the true history of the Confederacy.

But, overall, look at what happened. I heard him. He heard me. We talked honestly, and I must give him credit...

he truly *listened.* This is how progress is made. Listening to one another. No, it doesn't work in every instance, but it can work in many of them. It can work in your personal life and your workplaces. It is about our ability to hold space for the both/and while grounding on our collective humanity.

One of the things white supremacy does is place a protective force field around white people that they rarely have to leave. They can exist without encountering any challenges to it.

In 2021, Florida Governor Ron DeSantis pushed through a law called the "Stop WOKE Act." The law is designed to prevent people from talking about race or LGBTQ issues. Right-wing legislators and leaders in Texas, Pennsylvania, and Tennessee, among other places, have been attempting to ban the teachings of Martin Luther King, Jr. There are still significant swaths of white people who don't learn Black history, which is American history (Blow, 2022).

One expert on race, Dr. Kenneth V. Hardy, wrote in his book *The Enduring, Invisible, and Ubiquitous Centrality of Whiteness*:

"Speaking openly and honestly about race within racially integrated spaces is never easy; it is often marred by discomfort, defensiveness, coded language, and avoidance. These conversations become even more difficult when naming whiteness, especially in the presence of white people" (Hardy, 2021).

This is essentially what I was doing with the man sporting the Confederate drip. I challenged his sense of whiteness, and, to his credit, he responded with an open mind and change.

Will he keep his newfound sense of awareness? I don't know. What I do know is in the moment when I punctured his sense of white fragility—which is when a white person feels discomfort or even anger when confronted by information about racial inequality and injustice—and it was just me, a Black man, and this white man, talking respectfully and honestly, progress was made.

That's how progress will always be made. One or two people at a time.

THE FINAL WORD: What's clear to me is that in many cases, as my encounter with that man showed, once we each leave our fears and biases behind, there is room for us to communicate. We may not always agree but that's not the most important part. It's dealing respectfully with each other. There's also something else. We all must live with a common set of truths. He believed wearing Confederate gear was honoring the past when you cannot honor the shame that was slavery. If we have that common set of facts, we can truly begin to coexist.

Citations:

- Blow, C. M. (2022). *The Devil You Know: A Black Power Manifesto.*
- Coski, J. M. (2005). *The Confederate Battle Flag: America's Most Embattled Emblem.*
- Hardy, K. V. (2021). *The Enduring, Invisible, and Ubiquitous Centrality of Whiteness.*
- Janney, C. E. (2016). *Remembering the Civil War: Reunion and the Limits of Reconciliation.*
- McPherson, J. M. (1990). *Battle Cry of Freedom: The Civil War Era.*
- Vora, S. (2021). "What you need to know about the Confederate flag." *National Geographic.*

CHAPTER THREE:

THE WRINKLED SHIRT

My grandmother, Ertha Hopkins, taught me how to iron a shirt decades ago. I was in high school. She was highly proficient at ironing shirts because of what she did for a living. My grandmother was a nanny for a white family. She cleaned the house and took care of their two young children, and as part of her duties, she ironed a lot of shirts. Just before I entered high school my grandmother made a point to ensure I knew how to iron a dress shirt. It was important to her that a dress shirt looked proper, starched without wrinkle.

She was special, born on December 16, 1916, in Bamberg, S.C., to the late Tillman and Josephine (Cobbs) Bailey. Ertha, after her mother died, was raised by the Rev. Mattie J. Bailey, founder of Wheatfield Street College in York.

I remember her kindness and love, but I also came to view her teaching me how to iron wrinkled shirts meant more than the act itself. It came to represent a form of resentment. When I see someone with a wrinkled shirt, especially if that person is white, the story that shows up for me is *how dare you not iron that shirt especially when my grandmother was ironing shirts for people like you.*

I understand this isn't a logical or rational thing. But issues of race aren't always logical or rational.

One of the things we should do at this point is provide some sort of definition about what exactly racism is since it has come to mean so many different things to so many people.

Here is the strict definition: Racism refers to a belief that certain races are inherently superior or inferior to others, and results in discriminatory behavior or attitudes towards individuals based on their race (Bonilla-Silva, 1997).

However, as you likely know, and if not, you will learn, racism is much deeper than that definition. It can manifest in a variety of ways—not just occasionally, but daily—and it includes:

- **Microaggressions**: Everyday, subtle, and often unintentional acts of discrimination, such as making assumptions about someone's abilities or cultural norms based on their race (Sue et al., 2007).

- **Stereotyping**: Prejudiced beliefs about individuals based on their race, such as thinking all Black people are criminals (Devine, 1989).

- **Racial profiling**: The discriminatory practice of suspecting someone of criminal activity based solely on their race (Harris, 1999).

- **Employment and wage discrimination**: Unequal treatment in employment opportunities, pay, and promotion based on race (Pager, 2007).

- **Residential segregation**: The physical separation of different racial groups in communities, often due to historical and systemic racism (Massey & Denton, 1993).

I've grown and changed from where I was decades ago when I'd have those negative thoughts about a person I saw who had a wrinkled shirt. However, I must be honest. Sometimes that thinking still happens—just not as much. I'm always trying to be aware of my own bias, and I'm conscious that my personal story about the shirts, and the accompanying narrative, is impeding me from appreciating the human being. There's any number of reasons why that person had a wrinkled shirt. Maybe they had to leave for work in a rush because they were late.

I'm sure you understand by now what the wrinkled shirt represents. It's a symbol of the things Black people have endured, and continue to, just to exist. My grandmother took care of a white family to earn a paycheck and help take care of her family. She did it because she had to. There are plenty of white people who do jobs they don't want, but must, to earn a paycheck. Yet if you're Black, the efforts we must make in every part of our lives—from how we walk down the street, to how we avoid the police so that we don't end up dead—are processes that white people don't need to consider.

We'll discuss this more later in the book, but Black encounters with police are one of the ultimate moments of a wrinkled shirt. According to data from the Mapping Police Violence project, Black Americans are 2.5 times more likely than white Americans to be killed by police (Mapping Police Violence, 2023). In incidents of police violence where the race of the victim is known, Black individuals are more likely to be unarmed than white individuals. According to data from *The Washington Post*, in 2019, Black Americans accounted for 24% of unarmed individuals killed by police, despite making up only 13%

of the U.S. population (*The Washington Post*, 2019).

The culture of policing is so poisoned, particularly the policing of Black communities. Police officers are rarely charged or convicted for incidents of police violence. According to data from the National Police Misconduct Reporting Project, only about 1% of police officers involved in incidents of misconduct are ever convicted of a crime (NPMSRP, 2023). That, and the recruitment process as well as community engagement as it relates to policing, must change.

THE FINAL WORD: When my grandmother taught me to iron those wrinkled shirts, I never knew how much those moments would impact me years later. Those shirts became a symbol of defiance; and later would morph into something else, which was me looking inward to make sure I wasn't propagating the same type of stereotyping that I received from white people. My grandmother was loving and kind and taught me so much beyond those shirts.

Citations:

- Bonilla-Silva, E. (1997). Rethinking Racism: Toward a Structural Interpretation. *American Sociological Review*, 62(3), 465–480.
- Devine, P. G. (1989). Stereotypes and prejudice:

Their automatic and controlled components. *Journal of Personality and Social Psychology*, 56(1), 5–18.

- Harris, D. A. (1999). The Stories, the Statistics, and the Law: Why "Driving While Black" Matters. *Minnesota Law Review*, 84(2), 265–326.

- Massey, D. S., & Denton, N. A. (1993). *American Apartheid: Segregation and the Making of the Underclass.*

- Mapping Police Violence. (2023). *Mapping Police Violence Database.*

- NPMSRP. (2023). *National Police Misconduct Reporting Project.*

- Pager, D. (2007). The Use of Field Experiments for Studies of Employment Discrimination: Contributions, Critiques, and Directions for the Future. *Annals of the American Academy of Political and Social Science*, 609(1), 104–133.

- Sue, D. W., et al. (2007). Racial Microaggressions in Everyday Life: Implications for Clinical Practice. *American Psychologist*, 62(4), 271–286.

- *The Washington Post*. (2019). Police Shootings Database.

CHAPTER FOUR:

DEBT OWED

You may know the story of John Henry. If you don't, Henry was the mythical Black railroad worker, skilled with a mechanical drill, who in the late 1800s took on a machine in a track-building competition and died fighting that honorable battle against it. Henry was an allegory not just about the physical power of human beings, but also the intrusion of technology on 19th-century life. Wrote Jeanette Bicknell in *Reflections on John Henry: Ethical Issues in Singing Performance*:

"John Henry is a symbol of physical strength and endurance, of exploited labor, of the dignity of a human being against the degradations of the machine age, and of racial pride and solidarity. During World War II, his image was used in U.S. government propaganda as a symbol of social tolerance and diversity" (Bicknell, 2015).

The ballad has seen several incarnations, but its most common form goes like this:

When John Henry was a little baby,
Just a sittn' on his mammy's knee,
Said, "The Big Bend Tunnel on that C&O Road
Gonna be the death of me, Lord God
Going to be the death of me."
Well John Henry said to the Captain,
I'm gonna take a little trip downtown
Get me a thirty pound hammer with that nine foot
handle
I'll beat your steam drill down, Lord God
I'll beat your steam drill down.
Well John Henry hammered on that mountain
Till his hammer was striking fire
And the very last words that I heard that boy say
was
Cool drink of water 'for I die, Lord God
Cool drink of water 'for I die.
Well they carried him down to the graveyard
And they buried him in the sand

And every locomotive came a roarin' on by
They cried out, "There lies a steel drivin' man, Lord
God
There lies a steel drivin' man."
Well there's some say he came from Texas
There's some say he came from Maine
Well I don't give a damn where that poor boy was
from
You know that, he was a steel drivin' man, Lord
God
John Henry was a steel drivin' man.
Well when John Henry was a little baby,
Just a sittn' on his mammy's knee,
Said, "The Big Bend Tunnel on that C&O Road
Gonna be the death of me, Lord God
Going to be the death of me."

Yes, you may know the story of John Henry, but what you may not know is Henry likely wasn't just a tale. He was flesh and blood, and his story is part of the story of Blacks and reparations. The idea of reparations remains one of the thorniest topics in America today. I get asked about it all the time by white friends and clients. It's the subject of debates on news shows and in the workplace. It's a massive topic and one I want to get into here because it highlights one of the main points of this work: the devastating impact of ignored history and our responsibility to learn more of it. The question at hand is how to reconcile the financial harm that has been placed on a people? There is a debt owed with interest.

First, back to Henry. He lived in a post-emancipation America, where Southerners, no longer able to rely on free labor, had to invent other ways to monetize human suffering. One such way was prison labor and this, too, is where reparations come into play. Henry's story is part of this ugly time in American history and is important even now, all these years after his death.

There's a book called *Steel Drivin' Man* by Scott Reynolds Nelson. Nelson was one of several historians who believed that Henry was a real person who lived in the 1870s. Nelson's book says that Henry was a former Union soldier, imprisoned for theft while on a work assignment in Richmond, Virginia, and leased out with other inmates to blast tunnels through the Allegheny Mountains for the new Chesapeake & Ohio Railway (Nelson, 2006).

Nelson studied Southern railroads during Reconstruction, and he discovered an extraordinary number of convicts from the Virginia State Penitentiary that perished while constructing the C&O Railway. Nelson combined lines from the Henry ballad with facts he discovered on the ground. One line struck him:

"They took John Henry to the white house and buried him in the sand."

The main building of the penitentiary, he knew, was white. In 1992, while the prison was being demolished, workers had discovered some 300 skeletons. Nelson then looked through the state archives and found a prisoner named John William Henry. Henry's body was possibly one of those skeletons (Nelson, 2006).

As a *New York Times* review of Nelson's book notes, "Henry worked on the team assigned to drill the Lewis Tunnel in West Virginia, where steam drills were put to the test against workers with hammers. By 1874 he had disappeared from prison records, with no mention of pardon, parole or release, strongly suggesting that he died while working on the railroads and not inside the prison, where his death would have been recorded" (Allen, 2006).

The story added: "[Henry] was from New Jersey and, in some capacity, worked for the Union Army at City Point, a landing near Petersburg, Va., in 1866, when he was 18. In April of that year, he was arrested for stealing from a grocery store and sentenced to 10 years in prison. He was sent to the Virginia State Penitentiary, where the warden, desperate to raise revenue, had begun leasing prisoners to the railroad for 25 cents a day. John Henry was one."

Thus, in a remarkable stroke of irony, one of the few Black legends of mythology, who might turn out to be real, suffered a horrible death that had nothing to do with battling a machine, but instead was because of the abuses of that era in the South. Then, drilling machines churned up large amounts of silicon dust. This caused a lung disease called silicosis which was fatal and killed hundreds, if not thousands, of workers. In many cases, Black workers, like Henry.

This is real history. This is the history we all need to know. History should not be held back or manipulated based on an agenda. History must be taught, explored, and learned from to gain a deeper understanding of one another and this country.

The story of John Henry serves as an example of systemic exploitation. This exploitation—whether through slavery, convict leasing, or discriminatory policies—created a massive racial wealth gap.

‌—

Frederick Douglass was born a slave in Maryland. The year was 1818. Douglass was a rebel who fought his enslavement. One such act of rebellion was Douglass taught himself to read, and then secretly taught other enslaved people to read. Douglass escaped to New York and after overcoming an initial fear of public speaking, Douglass went on to become one of the anti-slavery movement's most eloquent speakers. Really, one of the most eloquent and passionate speakers in American history. He was also a prolific writer, penning his own autobiography, in addition to starting several abolitionist newspapers. Many abolitionists at the time were not supporters of women's rights, but Douglass was.

In 1863, during a speech at the Cooper Institute, Douglass told his audience of Black and white New Yorkers the reactions he saw of people after hearing of the Emancipation Proclamation.

"I never saw enthusiasm before," he recalled." I never saw joy before. Men, women, young and old, were up; hats and bonnets were in the air, and we had three cheers for Abraham Lincoln and three cheers for about everybody else."

But in 1880, with Reconstruction fully underway, came the stark realization that Black people had fought and earned their freedom, but reparations, monies, that should have been owed, weren't coming. As noted by intellectualists such as Nikole Hannah-Jones in the *1619 Project*, and other journalists, academics and scholars, the lack of reparations given then was the beginning of the cavernous racial wealth gap that would last to this day.

Today, the average white household has eight times the

wealth of the average Black household (*Federal Reserve Board Survey of Consumer Finances*, 2021). This gap is not about behavior or choices; it is about history. Specifically, how white people were able to create generational wealth off the backs of Black labor, often through theft and violence. Specifically, how white people were able to create a gigantic wealth lead off the backs of Black people for over 400 years. It's the equivalent of trying to catch the world's fastest marathoner after they get a 100-mile lead.

Whites didn't just steal freedom and lives; they stole property and burned down entire towns like Tulsa, Oklahoma, which was called the Black Wall Street. The federal government pushed highways through the middle of Black cities, destroying property values. Overall, whites stole generational wealth, and the loss of wealth is almost incalculable, likely trillions of dollars.

Let me explain.

At the conclusion of the Civil War, General William T. Sherman attended a meeting of Black leaders and asked them an important question: What do you want for your people? The leader of the delegation had a simple response: We want our own land so we can take care of ourselves. Less than a week later, Sherman issued Special Field Order 15. This is what most people now refer to as 40 Acres and a Mule. Sherman's order required the government to seize hundreds of thousands of acres from the Confederacy and split it among the newly emancipated people.

To this day, so many years later, Sherman's order remains the only, and I mean the only, effort made by this nation to compensate Blacks for centuries of slavery. And you know what happened next? Just months later, Abraham Lincoln was assassinated, and his successor, Andrew Johnson, a hardcore white supremacist, and slave owner, rescinded the order. Johnson returned the land to the same traitors who had fought against their own country (Foner, 1988).

Let's stop right here for a moment. Say we transport ourselves to an alternate universe where Lincoln wasn't assassinated, and Sherman's order stood. Maybe later white Southerners would have stolen the land back, but if they hadn't, that land now would be worth hundreds of billions of dollars. It likely would have been owned by Blacks for generations. This is, in fact, how whites created wealth: holding onto property for decades and centuries, that property accruing in value, or being sold for money, or having things built on it, increasing that value even more.

But back in our reality, that didn't happen.

In contrast, between 1862 and 1934, the federal government gave away 246 million acres of land to white families through the Homestead Act—land stolen from Indigenous peoples. Today, approximately 46 million white Americans, some 25 percent of the population, benefit from this generational wealth transfer (Gates, 2012).

When I talk about generational wealth, this is what I mean. Black people were cheated, and that cheating put us financially behind. That cheating was compounded by Jim Crow and countless other economic forms of discrimination lobbed at Black people like bombs for so, so long.

Thus, a bit of tough love for my white friends. If you're running a company, or are a member of a board, or even if you're just sitting in your living room watching television, and you wonder why Black people are behind economically, consider this: If you're honest with yourself, part of the answer is large swaths of wealth and land were stolen from Blacks and the Indigenous by whites. You, as a white person, and your ancestors, may have benefitted from these thefts.

How much money are we talking about that Blacks might be owed? Experts say if reparations were paid, the number would be in the trillions. Some say the number might be much higher. Several believe it is in the quadrillions of dollars. One quadrillion is 1,000 trillion dollars.

—

It is true that reparations are about money, about paying Black people what we're owed, but reparations are also about something else. They are about recognizing a wrong. In almost every aspect of American society, in many societies around the world, financial compensations for wrongs are commonplace. In the 1950s Germany did this following the atrocities of the Holocaust. "Germany has taken commendable steps to confront its role as the perpetrator of the Holocaust and to ensure that Holocaust victims and their heirs receive restitution and/or compensation," reads a recent U.S. Department of State report. "Germany also honors and remembers the victims of the Holocaust and has worked to cultivate a culture of remembrance. Its restitution measures range from compensating former owners and heirs for assets wrongfully seized during the Holocaust to making substantial financial contributions to victims' funds and survivors' pensions. From 1945 to 2018, the German government paid approximately $86.8 billion in restitution and compensation to Holocaust victims and their heirs (Bazyler & Alford, 2006). Germany has also identified Nazi-looted objects – including art works, books, and objects within larger collections – and has returned 16,000 objects to survivors and their heirs over the last 20 years."

1988, The U.S. Congress awarded $20,000 each to more than 80,000 Japanese Americans for their imprisonment during World War II. America also issued a long overdue apology.

The American government, unbelievably, even paid reparations to slave owners after the slaves were freed. That's right. Slave owners got paid. *Slave owners.*

The question I want you to think about is this: Why not Black people?

Why can't Black people be treated with that same type of respect?

Reparations, and history, are intrinsically intertwined. What we often forget is the attempt to ban, or limit, the teaching of history is equally part of the American ethos. After the Civil War, white Southerners attempted to rewrite history by casting the conflict as the South fighting Northern aggression and saying it wasn't about slavery, but the right to autonomy. Hundreds of years later that same lie exists in part because we never properly dealt with the Civil War in the same way that, say, Germany dealt with its horrors after the Nazis killed six million Jews and started a global conflict. In America, the Confederate flag is displayed in front yards.

A hundred years later, white politicians are still attempting to change or erase history. Florida Governor Ron DeSantis has brazenly created a legion of anti-Black legislation including banning advanced placement Black history. No other race in the state has had the teaching of its history banned except Black people. These actions reflect a long history of erasing Black contributions and struggles (Hannah-Jones, 2019).

The denial of reparations and the rewriting of history are intertwined. Without acknowledgment of the past, progress is impossible.

It doesn't stop with politicians. The right-wing media culture pushes anti-Black narratives of all kinds, but during Black History Month in 2023, there was a specific emphasis on denying Black history. In fact, as the organization Media Matters noted, Fox News ran an anti-Black segment on its various shows on each day of February in 2023. On Feb. 2, *The Story with Martha MacCallum,* guest and right-wing podcast host Dave Rubin defended DeSantis' rejection of the College Board's Advanced Placement African American Studies course by accusing public schools of teaching "neoracism," stating, "No one should be taught that your skin color does matter, and your skin color is the thing that should get you ahead whether it's at a college admission…or whether it's to get the job or the grad school situation after that. But that is exactly what they want to teach. So, DeSantis is really just saying enough is enough."

Then on Feb. 3, On *One Nation with Brian Kilmeade,* The Heartland Institute's Peter Wood claimed *The 1619 Project* book is "a shameless compilation of misstatements, misrepresentations of the American past... This book is mainly aimed at provoking, more or less, despair on the part of African Americans and guilt on the part of white Americans." Host Brian Kilmeade called *The 1619 Project* Hulu series a "disgraced and dishonest" project, "an affront to history itself," and "historical fiction masquerading as fact," warning that "no part of our history seems safe; no hero is left untarnished."

During *The Five,* on Feb. 7, co-host Jesse Waters suggested that the people "who financed" and "designed" slavery deserve credit for American infrastructure built by slaves. Watters also joked that he should receive reparations for being "one percent Black."

On and on it went. On and on it goes still.

One thing I constantly think about, and this is true regarding reparations and beyond, is that Black people must relentlessly fight, because the people who hate us, and want us to suffer, never stop. Their playbook never changes. From George Wallace to Ron DeSantis, and many others, they utilize what has been done for centuries: the use of fear, false safety concerns, and fear of loss of societal power and status, to keep Black people ostracized and powerless. They have and continue to attack our housing, healthcare, jobs, recreational spaces, voting rights, education, equitable justice under the law, the pursuit of happiness, and even things like access to healthy food and water. The cycle has not changed. That's why Black people constantly fight. Any moment of relaxation can lead to losing rights or even our lives.

THE FINAL WORD: I have to say that despite the ugliness around us, what I've always been heartened by is that there are a significant number of white people who don't tolerate hate and are allies in the fight against historical erasure (and racism overall). One of them is the most powerful man in the free world.

In 1915, as the *New York Times* notes, President Woodrow Wilson watched *The Birth of a Nation*, which is essentially a recruitment video for the Ku Klux Klan, in the East Room of the White House with a small group of people. It was certainly a low moment, but over a century later, in the same room, President Joe Biden showed the movie *Till,* about the 14-year-old Black child murdered in 1955 that helped to propel the modern civil rights movement.

Biden had gathered families of people killed in hate crimes. He had a message for them:

"History matters," he told the small crowd. "We should know everything about our history, and that's what great nations do."

As I again remind you to journal your thoughts, I want to also remind you to pay attention to the world around you. How is it changing and most importantly why is it changing? Explore these reasons, educate yourself with credible media sources, and don't let ignorance or hatred be a guide. What role can you play in ensuring that change leads to justice and equity for all?

Citations:

- Allen, R. (2006). "Book Review: Steel Drivin' Man." *The New York Times.*
- Bazyler, M. J., & Alford, R. P. (2006). *Holocaust Restitution: Perspectives on the Litigation and Its Legacy.*
- Bicknell, J. (2015). *Reflections on John Henry: Ethical Issues in Singing Performance.*
- Federal Reserve Board Survey of Consumer Finances. (2021).
- Foner, E. (1988). *Reconstruction: America's Unfinished Revolution, 1863-1877.*
- Gates, H. L. Jr. (2012). "Who Got America's Land?" *The Root.*
- Hannah-Jones, N. (2019). *The 1619 Project.*

- Nelson, S. R. (2006). *Steel Drivin' Man: John Henry, the Untold Story of an American Legend*.

CHAPTER FIVE

YES, HOPE CAN WORK

During the pandemic, I facilitated a workshop on bias and power, afterwards debriefed with the area leader. We had a great conversation about the content and his plans to move the initiative forward throughout his organization. I was impressed with his plan. At one point in the conversation, he said something that surprised me.

"I have to set clear objective criteria because hope is not a strategy," he explained.

I have to say the comment caught me off guard. I was triggered because I thought it was a jab at Obama's "HOPE and Change" or Jessie Jackson's motto of "Keep Hope Alive."

His comment implied that hope was for suckers, that hope was something trivial. I didn't ask for clarity because I knew I was not in a place for generative dialogue. I didn't circle back on that comment.

About a week later, I was delivering the content again, and another area leader kicked off the session and made a similar comment.

"Hope is not a strategy, and we need you to focus on how you're going to implement change after this session," he said.

So again, I was triggered at the start of the session because of the leader's comment about hope.

I can have reactions tied to the amygdala, fight! If you come at me, I'm coming back at you harder. But I've learned over time that my initial response is sometimes not the best option. The amygdala is part of the brain responsible for processing emotions, particularly fear and anger. It activates the "fight, flight, or freeze" response when a perceived threat arises (LeDoux, 2000).

Catching my breath, centering myself, and being intentional about my actions is often the best way to honor myself. It allows space for peace, gratitude, and connection (Siegel, 2010).

So, can hope be a strategy?

I link hope to faith and courage. Faith is the belief in something unseen (Hebrews 11:1, New International Version). Courage is about connection to the heart during uncertainty.

The opposites of hope are fear and anxiety. Fear is the terror of the unknown. Or, to put it another way, it's false thoughts and visions of the unknown and/or "other" that appear real (Achor, 2010).

When that manager said "hope is not a strategy," he likely wasn't talking about me or Obama or anyone else. It's probably a saying he uses that caught on with other people in the company.

I reacted to what he said with irritation because to me, hope isn't trivial, and in some ways, it *can* be a strategy. It's a way to move forward into the unknown with love and compassion.

Hope as a strategy isn't about wishful thinking. It's about leveraging a vision of what's possible to inspire action. Positive psychology defines hope as a belief that one can find pathways to desired goals and become motivated to use those pathways (Snyder, 2002).

Dr. Martin Luther King Jr. once said:

"We must accept finite disappointment, but never lose infinite hope" (King, 1963).

Hope can create a foundation for resilience and change. A study in *Psychological Science* found that hopeful people are better at problem-solving and coping with setbacks (Rand & Cheavens, 2009).

The unknown should not be feared; instead, it should be respected and honored. We could consider this an opportunity to connect and grow. To be innovative and build community.

Even when things seem terrible, I will always have hope, especially for all of us, for our collective humanity.

THE FINAL WORD: Hope, faith, and courage are interconnected. They empower us to face uncertainty with resilience and purpose. While hope alone may not create change, it can inspire the vision and determination necessary to act.

Citations:

- Achor, S. (2010). *The Happiness Advantage: How a Positive Brain Fuels Success in Work and Life.*
- Hebrews 11:1. New International Version (NIV).
- King, M. L. Jr. (1963). *Strength to Love.*
- LeDoux, J. E. (2000). *The Emotional Brain: The Mysterious Underpinnings of Emotional Life.*
- Rand, K. L., & Cheavens, J. S. (2009). Hope theory: A member of the positive psychology

family. *Handbook of Positive Psychology*.

- Siegel, D. J. (2010). *Mindsight: The New Science of Personal Transformation*.

- Snyder, C. R. (2002). Hope theory: Rainbows in the mind. *Psychological Inquiry*, 13(4), 249–275.

CHAPTER SIX

THE INVISIBLE HEROES

In high school, I became pretty good at hurdling, starring on the track team. However, it took me years to get good at it, and there were a number of crashes with both the hurdles and the ground. So, my track coach gave me a piece of advice: *Take the hurdle home and practice.*

That's what I did. Leaping over it, falling over it, crashing into it...sometimes all three simultaneously. The practice, though, was constant, and eventually, that hurdle wasn't the formidable barrier that it was when I first attempted to launch over it. That hurdle became my way to overcome and truly express myself. *Put your chest into it*, I'd tell myself.

The hurdle today is weather beaten and in a rough state. Decades later, I keep it around, maybe as a symbol, maybe as a piece of nostalgia. Once, my finger caught between two of the hurdle's metal pieces, giving me a good slice. It was a reminder that the barrier can still have impact.

That hurdle took me far. I eventually ran track at Fairleigh Dickinson University where I was a two-time Northeast Conference champion in the 55-meter hurdles—first winning the gold in 1988. I helped my school win two team titles in the NEC Men's Indoor Track and Field Championships. I also qualified twice for the NCAA Championships, once outdoors in 1989 and a trip indoors the following year. As a freshman, I won the 60-meter hurdles titles at the Metropolitan and New Jersey Championships. I was inducted in the school's Hall of Fame in 2022.

One of the big things my heroes all have in common is that ability to get up after falling. It's how I've lived my life. It sounds cliché but it's vital to keep that perspective. It's vital to never forget the life lessons those hurdles teach you. It could be falling while hurdling or getting hit with an egg. Catch your breath, get your wits about you and move forward.

We talked about history earlier and how some politicians and others want to eradicate learning about it. The reason for this is extremely tactical. If you erase history, you erase accountability. If you erase accountability, you remove any chance of reparations. But mostly, eliminating history eliminates the strength of the oppressed. The Indigenous population survived biological warfare from colonizers using smallpox as a weapon, and centuries of murder (Stannard, 1993). Black people survived over 400 years of slavery and a century of Jim Crow. There is remarkable strength in surviving, and to survive, you need heroes. There is a legion of heroes throughout Black history. But there's a problem.

Most people don't know who those heroes are.

For so many people, Black history starts with slavery and ends with Martin Luther King Jr. There's not much more between those two—or after. There are thousands of Black heroes who don't appear in many history books. They are forgotten or appear in snippets in commercials between quarters of an NFL game during Black History Month.

There are five people I wanted to introduce you to. These are only a handful of many, but the point is to show that Black history is rich and full of heroes who don't make history books, and even worse, there are governors and right-wing leaders who want to erase these heroes from existence.

But you cannot erase from history people so skilled at mastering those hurdles.

GLORIA RICHARDSON

There's an iconic photo that I bet you've never seen. It's during a 1963 protest in Cambridge, Maryland, and a soldier is holding a rifle with a bayonet attached. The bayonet is just inches away from the face of a Black woman, and in the photo, she is pushing the weapon—and the deadly, protruding bayonet—away from her face. The woman standing up to that soldier is Gloria Richardson (Joseph, 2006).

Richardson has been called one of the unsung heroes of the Civil Rights movement. She's been called a silent warrior and a general because of her tenacity and refusal to stop fighting for the rights of Black people in that era and since.

The fight for civil rights wasn't just relegated to the hot spots in the Deep South like Birmingham. They also took place in cities like Cambridge—just as segregated and problematic but far away from the perceived front lines. The state of Maryland, in fact, may have been more of an outpost in the civil rights era, and a forgotten one, but the fights there were just as bloody and vicious as almost any other place.

In Cambridge, there was a street literally called Race St. that divided the town's Black and white populations. Housing in the city was so bad, and so segregated, that some Black residents lived in places that were actual chicken coops, as Richardson said in a 2011 interview with the Library of Congress. The Black community faced constant violence including from white members of the National Guard. On some nights, soldiers would drive through neighborhoods in military vehicles shooting machine guns into the homes of Black citizens. Fortunately, no one was hurt or killed, she explained.

It was later confirmed that Richardson's phone was tapped, like many other civil right leaders. I often wonder what our current state would be if time and money was spent on healing our communities vs conspiring against civil rights leaders.. The money and energy could have been used to solve the root cause issues facing our communities and the overall civil rights concerns.

Hundreds of people took part in protests to desegregate restaurants and other places in Cambridge. Those protests lasted for months, and Richardson was one of the organizers. Her campaign was so effective that in 1963 she helped broker a treaty with Attorney General Robert Kennedy called The Treaty of Cambridge (Joseph, 2006). It guaranteed the desegregation of housing, schools, hospitals and other areas in and around the city. It's considered one of the landmark achievements of the era. One year later she would work with Malcolm X to create an organization that would fight for Black liberation.

ALTHEA GIBSON

There are few athletes in the history of American sports who had more impact than Althea Gibson. If there was a Mount Rushmore of Black athletes, she'd be on it alongside potential names such as Muhammad Ali, Jackie Robinson, Jesse Owens (who won four gold medals in the 1936 Olympics with Hitler in the stands watching), and Colin Kaepernick. There can be a debate about Kaepernick being on the Mount Rushmore of black athletes, but Gibson's life is the material of Hollywood movies and in many places, she's been ignored or forgotten.

Gibson's career in both tennis and golf was marked by extraordinary talent, perseverance, and a fierce determination to succeed in the face of racism and discrimination. This is the common denominator among many of these heroes—they hit stunning heights with the anchor of racism tied around their waist. Imagine jumping over a hurdle with bricks attached to your feet.

Gibson was born in 1927, in Silver, South Carolina. She was the eldest of five children, and her family moved to Harlem when she was young. Growing up, Gibson was a gifted athlete who excelled in a variety of sports, including basketball and track and field. It wasn't until she was introduced to tennis at the age of 14 that she found her true calling. Despite her talent, Gibson faced significant obstacles in pursuing that sport. At the time, tennis was almost entirely segregated, with few opportunities for Black athletes to compete at the highest levels. Gibson was forced to play in a segregated league for Black players, and even then, she struggled to find consistent opportunities to compete. She eventually caught the attention of a Black doctor named Hubert Eaton, who became her mentor and helped her to improve her game.

In 1949, Gibson entered her first major tournament, the National Negro Championships, and won both the singles and doubles titles. The following year, she was the first Black player to compete in the U.S. National Championships (now known as the U.S. Open). Despite facing significant racism and discrimination from both players and fans, Gibson advanced to the second round of the tournament. It was common throughout her career to be called racial slurs not just by the fans, but also from opponents. She was also occasionally spat on by spectators.

Over the next several years, Gibson's fame continued to rise. She won the National Negro Championships again in 1950 and 1951, and in 1952, she won her first major international title at the Caribbean Championships. In 1953, she made history once again by becoming the first

Black woman to play at Wimbledon, where she advanced to the quarterfinals. But it was in 1956 that Gibson truly made her mark on the sport. That year, she won the French Championships (now known as the French Open), becoming the first Black player to win a Grand Slam title. She followed up that victory with a win at Wimbledon, becoming the first Black player to win that tournament as well. She also won the U.S. Championships that year, completing a historic sweep of the sport's major titles.

Gibson continued to compete at the highest levels of tennis for several more years, winning the U.S. Championships again in 1957 and 1958. But despite her success, she faced ongoing discrimination and racism. She was often denied access to hotels and restaurants while on tour, and she was barred from certain tournaments because of her race. In 1959, Gibson retired from tennis at the age of 32. She briefly pursued a career in music, but eventually turned to golf. In 1964, she became the first Black woman to play on the Ladies Professional Golf Association (LPGA) tour, and she competed in a total of 171 LPGA events over the course of her career (Krane, 2005).

After retiring from golf in the early 1970s, Gibson became a tennis coach and advocate for young athletes. She was inducted into two Halls of Fame: in 1971 the International Tennis Hall of Fame, and nine years later the International Women's Sports Hall of Fame. She also received the Presidential Medal of Freedom in 1991. Billie Jean King, herself a legend, said of Gibson: "She was a pioneer and opened the doors for all of us" (Krane, 2005).

ABRAHAM GALLOWAY

There may be no one who exemplifies the phenomenon of forgotten history than a man named Abraham Galloway. Galloway was a pioneering Black activist who fought for civil rights and social justice during the Reconstruction Era in the United States. Born into slavery in North Carolina in 1837, Galloway was able to escape and eventually became a key figure in the fight for racial equality in the South. If you asked most people who Galloway was, they wouldn't know.

As a child, Galloway was sold away from his mother and siblings and forced to work on a plantation. He eventually escaped and fled to the North, where he became involved in the abolitionist movement. During the Civil War, Galloway returned to the South and worked as a spy and recruiter for the Union army, helping to enlist thousands of Black soldiers.

Thus, Galloway didn't just escape and enjoy his freedom, which would have been entirely justifiable. Instead, he got his freedom and came back to fight for the freedom of others.

After the war, Galloway continued his activism, working to secure political and civil rights for all Black people, both enslaved and free. He played a key role in the formation of the North Carolina Republican Party (which, at the time, more closely aligned with abolitionists) and was elected to the state legislature in 1868. During his time in office, he fought for public education, land reform, and voting rights for Black citizens. Galloway faced intense racism and hostility from white Democrats, who sought to limit the power of Black politicians and strip away their rights. Galloway was forced to flee the state at one point after being threatened with violence, but he continued to fight for justice and equality throughout his life.

Galloway also played a role in the fight for voting rights. Galloway helped to draft North Carolina's first state constitution, which provided for universal suffrage and the right to hold public office (Crow, 1989). Galloway's work laid the groundwork for the Voting Rights Act of 1965, which finally secured the right to vote for Blacks throughout the country.

What you see with Galloway is how his contributions to the fight for civil rights were immense, yet his story has been largely overlooked in textbooks and popular culture. Galloway was a visionary who saw a future where Black men and women could live free and equal lives, and he worked tirelessly to make that vision a reality. His legacy lives on in the struggles of activists today who continue to fight for racial and social justice. As civil rights leader Julian Bond once said of Galloway: "His life and work inspire us to continue the struggle for a more just and equitable society."

DAISY BATES

Many people may know the Little Rock Nine, a group of Black students who faced virulent and horrific opposition when they tried to integrate Central High School in Little Rock, Arkansas. What many don't know is that a group of activists and journalists spent months preparing those brave Black kids for the moment and the ugliness they would endure. Those teenagers needed a support system, and the bedrock foundation of their support was Daisy Bates.

There's an iconic photo of Bates that isn't in most schoolbooks. Bates is on the phone speaking to moms to convince them to send their children into harm's way. Think about that for a moment. You want to give segregation a death blow but to do it, you need parents to trust you, and Bates was able to earn that trust.

As MSNBC analyst Joy Reid told *Esquire* in 2018: "What can one say about Daisy Bates? It's shameful that she's so little known. There's no Little Rock Nine without her. Think about this: these were school children. She had to get mothers to be okay with their children integrating a hostile environment, where other adults would be screaming at them. It's unthinkable. My favorite photo of her is the one where she's on the phone with all the moms —— the small t, small p 'tea party,' where mothers were forming a phone tree to protect the lives of these nine kids. Really, the bravest kids ever. Daisy Bates was in charge of this integration effort, and she should be remembered for it."

In the late 1950s and early 1960s, Bates had a personal connection to the struggle for civil rights in the United States. Her husband, Lucius Christopher Bates, was a civil rights activist and journalist who had been a mentor to NAACP leader Medgar Evers. In 1952, the couple moved to Little Rock, where they began publishing a newspaper called the *Arkansas State Press*. The paper focused on issues of racial justice and became a powerful voice for the Black community in the state.

In 1957, when the Little Rock Nine attempted to integrate Central High School, Bates played a crucial role in organizing support for the students. She worked closely with NAACP lawyers and leaders, including Thurgood Marshall, to prepare the students for the challenges they would face. She also helped to coordinate a network of volunteers who provided protection and assistance to the students as they attended school. Despite their efforts, the Little Rock Nine faced intense opposition from white segregationists, who staged protests, riots, and acts of violence to block their entry into the school. Bates was herself the target of threats and harassment, and her newspaper was firebombed in 1959. Despite the dangers, she wasn't intimidated.

In 1958, Bates was elected president of the Arkansas State Conference of the NAACP, becoming the first woman to hold the position (Reed, 1998). She used her platform to continue advocating for racial justice and played a key role in efforts to desegregate public facilities and improve voting rights for Black citizens in the state. She was, in short, a hero and to this day, one who should be much better known.

VIOLA LIUZZO

Viola Liuzzo was a courageous and passionate civil rights activist who gave her life in the fight for racial equality. Her murder in 1965 shocked the nation. Liuzzo, who was white, is also an example of what can happen to allies who back Black people fighting racism.

Born Viola Gregg in 1925 in California, she grew up in a middle-class family and attended college at age 16. She later married and had five children, settling in Detroit, Michigan, where she became involved in the civil rights movement. Liuzzo was a committed activist who worked with the NAACP and participated in local protests and demonstrations.

In 1965, Liuzzo traveled to Selma, Alabama, to take part in the historic Selma to Montgomery voting rights march. Liuzzo was deeply committed to this cause, and saw her participation in the march as a crucial part of her work as a civil rights activist.

After the march, Liuzzo was driving a Black activist named Leroy Moton to the Montgomery airport when she was followed and then shot by Ku Klux Klan members. She was killed instantly, while Moton survived by pretending to be dead. Four men were arrested and charged with her murder, including one who turned out to be an FBI informant. Her murder was intended to send a message to not just Black people, but to whites, that if they joined the fight to help Black people they, too, would be targeted (FBI, 2006).

In the years since Liuzzo's death, there have been efforts to honor her memory and recognize her contributions to the civil rights movement. In 2018, a highway in Michigan was named after her, and a documentary film about her life and death was released in 2019. Liuzzo, however, remains one of those mostly unknown names.

—

This list of invisible heroes goes on and on and on...

Why, again, am I giving history lessons? Janai Nelson, president and director-counsel of the Legal Defense Fund, said it well in an editorial in the *New York Times*. Nelson was writing of attacks on Black history, and to me, those attacks would lead to even more burying of Black heroes in history than now.

"The losses to our nation, if this broad attack on our shared history is allowed to continue, are incalculable," Nelson wrote. "Not only will it breed a generation of Americans indoctrinated by ignorance; it will deny them the analytical skills to understand the complex history of this experimental democracy, as well as the historical grounding to sustain it. Students will arrive at institutions of higher learning wholly ill equipped to engage with the historical foundations of this country, which include and are inextricable from the history of Black Americans. Moreover, it will deny future generations the full story of turmoil and triumph that is America" (Nelson, 2023).

THE FINAL WORD: If these heroes' stories are forgotten or erased, people who fight the good fight, like my mother, will be forgotten, and their legacies obliterated. This is no longer a theory. This is real. We are seeing attempts across the nation, with the state of Florida leading the way, to erase Black history. I would urge you, that as you journal your own thoughts, read about what's happening. It's important to be educated about all of this.

Citations:

- Crow, J. J. (1989). *Black Reconstruction in North Carolina*. UNC Press.
- FBI. (2006). "Viola Liuzzo: Civil Rights Martyr." *FBI Vault*.
- Joseph, P. E. (2006). *Waiting 'Til the Midnight Hour: A Narrative History of Black Power in America*.
- Krane, V. (2005). *Playing With Fire: Women Athletes of the 20th Century*.
- Nelson, J. (2023). "Don't Let Them Erase Black History." *The New York Times*.
- Reed, R. (1998). *The Little Rock Nine: Struggle for Integration*.
- Stannard, D. E. (1993). *American Holocaust: The Conquest of the New World*.

CHAPTER SEVEN

THE THIN BLACK AND BLUE LINE

When I was growing up in Maryland, like so many other Black people, I was stopped by the police. For a broken taillight that wasn't broken. For speeding when I wasn't. Sometimes, a reason wasn't even given. A dozen stops, at least, and none of them legitimate. Not one. Again, this isn't just my story. This is the story of many Black and brown people in America.

I despised those stops. Of course, no one wants to

be stopped by police, but there's something particularly humiliating about being stopped when you know it's happening because of the color of your skin. It's infuriating and it becomes even more so when it happens to your son.

My oldest, Kalil, was driving with three other friends, all football players like him, in a Maryland beach area. They were pulled over by police. Everyone in the car was Black and the officers were white.

The police asked everyone to get out of the car and show identification. I'm in my mid-fifties, have been pulled over a number of times, and not once was I ever asked to get out of the car.

My son and his friends were held for approximately 45 minutes and then let go. They were never given an explanation. They weren't ticketed or even given a warning for anything.

It wouldn't have justified what happened, but my son wasn't even driving a new or expensive car. It was an older Volkswagen Jetta.

It's clear what happened. Someone saw a car full of Black kids, driving on a local road, in a beach area that doesn't normally have a lot of Black beachgoers, and called the police. It was racism, and the police obliged.

I was furious. I contacted the department where the officers were from and got a startling response. I was told there was no record of that stop.

If you think what happened to me or my son is unusual, you haven't been paying attention. We were lucky. So much worse has happened between some Black people and the police. One particularly egregious example of police abusing power involved a young, Black medical worker in Louisville, Kentucky named Breonna Taylor.

Several years after the botched raid by the Louisville Metro Police Department that led to Taylor's death—a death that happened while she was simply just existing in her apartment—Attorney General Merrick Garland, in March of 2023, presented a devastating report that showed just how deep the rot went inside the Louisville Metro Police Department (LMPD). The 90-page report from the Justice Department exhumed a police department that was out of control and targeted Black citizens more than any other group (DOJ, 2023).

"For years, LMPD has practiced an aggressive style of policing that it deploys selectively, especially against Black people, but also against vulnerable people throughout the city," the report noted (DOJ, 2023).

"LMPD cites people for minor offenses, like wide turns and broken taillights, while serious crimes like sexual assault and homicide go unsolved," the report added. "Some officers demonstrate disrespect for the people they are sworn to protect. Some officers have videotaped themselves throwing drinks at pedestrians from their cars; insulted people with disabilities; and called Black people 'monkeys,' 'animal,' and 'boy.'"

The report found that the LMPD:

- Uses excessive force, including unjustified neck restraints and unreasonable use of police dogs and tasers.
- Conducts searches based on invalid warrants.
- Unlawfully executes warrants without knocking and announcing.
- Unlawfully stops, searches, detains and arrests people during traffic and pedestrian stops.
- Violates the rights of people engaged in protected speech critical of policing.
- Discriminates against people with behavioral health disabilities while responding to crises.

Police abuse is a plague, occurring from coast to coast, sea to shining sea. The examples are numerous. They occur in large departments like Los Angeles and New York and in small ones like East Cleveland, Ohio. There, in the Ohio department, at one point in 2023, more than a third of the officers were indicted for alleged public corruption and civil rights violations, with many of the incidents caught on video (Weaver, 2023).

One particularly awful video showed officers stomping on the head of a handcuffed man and repeatedly using their stun guns on him.

There are, of course, other examples, like the killing of Eric Garner in 2014. Garner died after being placed in a chokehold by a New York City police officer, despite Garner's pleas that he could not breathe. Philando Castile was shot and killed in 2016 by a police officer during a traffic stop in Falcon Heights, Minnesota. The officer claimed he feared for his life, but Castile was licensed to carry a firearm and had informed the officer of that fact. There was also the massacre of MOVE members in 1985. The Philadelphia Police Department dropped a bomb on the home of the MOVE organization, a group of Black activists, killing 11 people and destroying dozens of homes in the neighborhood. Yes, the police literally dropped a bomb on an entire neighborhood.

Do communities, all communities, need some type of protect and serve? Yes, absolutely. But what's also needed is the police seeing people as human beings, not things to be corralled. There's a question that must be asked, and every police officer needs to answer it.

Can every cop, and police department, acknowledge the history of policing, and how that history impacts policing today?

Because, well, that history is ugly.

There is a basic truth that we must accept when we talk about police abuse. Much of it, if not all, traces back to slavery. Back to the fear slave owners had that one day the slaves would rebel. That fear came true in 1791 in what is now modern-day Haiti. The French enslaved approximately 500,000 Africans, and when they rebelled, the slaves burned down almost every plantation on the island. The *1619 Project* says those enslaved people became the first in the *history of the world* to successfully overthrow their enslavers and create their own nation. Just thirteen years after that revolution, they founded Haiti, which was the world's first Black Republic. They also became the first nation in the Americas to abolish slavery.

Historians maintain that the existence of a nation so close to America, which overthrew its oppressors and abolished slavery, caused fear among slaveholders in this country that what happened in Haiti could happen here.

So during, and particularly after, the uprising in Haiti, slave owners in America initiated a series of laws and actions to crack down on the enslaved population. Those actions would produce grotesque tentacles that would reach into the 21st century. At the time, the codes limited the movement of Black people, prevented Black people from owning weapons of any kind—not just firearms, but anything that could be utilized as a weapon. Blacks were also prevented from assembling and even worshiping.

There was a law passed in Charleston, South Carolina—and I'm not making this up—which prevented enslaved and free Black people from singing or dancing. There was, in effect, a law against Black joy.

To explain this history, I turn again to the *1619 Project*, a work that is often demonized by the right, but one that provides immeasurable help to digest America's past. One part of that history, as the project explains, is that slave owners needed a way to enforce all these laws and restrictions on Black life (including Black happiness), and this is where the beginnings of policing in America truly starts. This is where the slave patrols come in, and what happened in the past, impacts the present.

These patrols were tasked with enforcing slave codes and controlling the movements and behavior of enslaved people. This included the use of surveillance, harassment, and violence to maintain white supremacy (Hadden, 2001). Slave patrols would often conduct random searches of enslaved people's homes, and they would frequently stop and question Black people who were not enslaved.

When slavery was abolished in 1865, the responsibilities of the slave patrols were transferred to law enforcement officers. This is where the past prologue comes into play.

During the Reconstruction era, Southern states

created the Black Codes. Their main purpose was to restrict the freedoms of newly freed Black people. These codes allowed law enforcement officers to arrest Black people for minor offenses, such as loitering and vagrancy, and force them to work without pay on chain gangs (Du Bois, 1935).

The Black Codes were eventually struck down by the Supreme Court, but they were followed by Jim Crow laws that were designed to maintain the racial hierarchy that had been established during slavery. Jim Crow enforced segregation and discrimination against Black people, and they were enforced by law enforcement officers.

In the 1960s, the Civil Rights Movement led to the passage of federal laws that prohibited discrimination based on race, color, religion, sex, or national origin. However, despite these laws, systemic racism and bias persisted in law enforcement.

In the years since the Civil Rights Movement, law enforcement officers have continued to use the tactics and strategies that were employed by slave patrols to control and subjugate Black people. These tactics include racial profiling, stop and frisk, and aggressive use of force (Alexander, 2010).

The impact of slave patrols on modern policing is significant. The tactics and strategies that were employed by slave patrols have been passed down through generations of law enforcement officers. The use of these tactics has contributed to a pattern of systemic racism and bias in modern-day policing. Law enforcement officers act as agents of social control, rather than protectors of public safety. This has contributed to a widespread lack of trust between law enforcement and communities of color and has perpetuated deep-seated racial inequalities in the criminal justice system.

How much does the legacy of white supremacy in policing still factor into today's law enforcement universe? A 2006 FBI assessment warned of the threat of white nationalism in policing. Reuters reported in 2022 that the presence of white supremacists, and aligned beliefs, in American law enforcement is still pervasive.

—

I told you this conversation wouldn't be easy. But you need to know all that history. There can't be solutions without understanding the past, and thankfully, there are potential solutions.

First, we need to start at the source. We should examine the training associated with helping officers manage their own trauma—personal, professional and institutional. Imagine if I never learned how to process trauma and I encountered a challenging call. How might that trauma show up at home and on the job? The top killer of police the last few years is Covid-19. The second-biggest cause of law enforcement death? Suicide.

Second, there's a blueprint for law enforcement to follow. On December 18, 2014, President Barack Obama pushed the country to a better place with a significant executive order. It established the Task Force on 21st Century Policing. The task force came up with six pillars:

1. Community engagement and partnership: This pillar emphasizes the importance of building strong relationships and partnerships between law enforcement agencies and the communities they serve. It involves working collaboratively with community members to identify and address crime and public safety issues.

2. Crime prevention and reduction: Focuses on strategies to prevent and reduce crime, such as proactive policing, targeted enforcement, and crime analysis. It involves using data and intelligence to identify patterns and trends and developing interventions to address them.

3. Proactive policing and problem-solving: This stresses the importance of proactive policing, which involves identifying and addressing underlying conditions and risk factors that contribute to crime and disorder. It involves using problem-solving

strategies to address specific issues, rather than simply reacting to incidents as they occur.

4. Professionalism and ethics: Maintain high standards of professionalism and ethical behavior among law enforcement officers. It involves providing ongoing training and education, as well as accountability and transparency in all aspects of policing.

5. Innovation and technology: Use technology and innovative approaches to improve policing. It involves leveraging tools like data analytics, social media, and community-based surveillance to enhance public safety and improve police effectiveness.

6. Officer wellness and safety: Support the health and safety of law enforcement officers. It involves providing resources and support for physical and mental wellness, as well as ensuring that officers have the necessary equipment and training to perform their duties safely and effectively (COPS Office, 2015).

The taskforce recommendations are important, but I also wanted to list my own, which I think are more practical. They are:

1. Implement Implicit Bias Training: Police departments can provide training that helps officers

identify and acknowledge their own biases and how they may affect their behavior on the job.

2. Increase Diversity: Police departments should prioritize recruiting and hiring more officers from diverse backgrounds, including people of color, women, and members of other marginalized communities.

3. Strengthen Accountability: Police departments should hold officers accountable for their actions by establishing clear policies and procedures for reporting and investigating misconduct, and by ensuring that officers who engage in discriminatory behavior are held responsible.

4. Enhance Community Policing: Departments can adopt community policing strategies that prioritize building trust and collaboration with communities, and that involve officers working closely with residents and community organizations to identify and address local issues. Work with people in the community that are credible messengers.

5. Limit Use of Force: Police departments can adopt policies that limit the use of force and prioritize de-escalation tactics in situations where force is necessary.

6. Implement Body Cameras: Police departments can require officers to wear body cameras that record

all interactions with the public, which can provide an objective record of police interactions and help hold officers accountable for their actions. This is of course a good idea, but we've seen that it's far from a panacea. Officers were wearing body cams when Nichols was beaten to death. It doesn't mean police shouldn't wear them. It does mean, however, that like these other solutions, they are only one of many measures needed to bring change.

7. Increase Transparency: Departments can be more transparent by publishing data on police practices, including use of force, traffic stops, and arrests, which can help identify patterns of discrimination.

8. Promote Alternatives to Incarceration: Departments can work with community organizations and local governments to develop alternatives to incarceration that prioritize rehabilitation and support for individuals and families affected by the criminal justice system.

9. Reform Police Culture: Departments can work to change the culture of policing by promoting empathy, compassion, and respect for all members of the community.

10. Address Systemic Racism: Ultimately, fixing racism in policing requires addressing the broader systemic issues that contribute to racial

inequality, including unequal access to education, employment, and housing, as well as the history of racial discrimination in the criminal justice system.

⊷

When President Biden gave his State of the Union speech in February of 2023, cameras caught members of the Congressional Black Caucus wearing a black pin with the number "1870" on it. To commemorate the first known police killing of a free Black person. Henry Truman, a 26-year-old Black man, was shot by a Philadelphia officer for allegedly shoplifting. The pins were a call for action on reforming the institution of policing. Since 1870, thousands of Black people have been killed by police, including over 1,300 since 2017 (Statista, 2023).

The incident Congresspeople were memorializing happened on March 31, 1870, when 26-year-old Henry Truman, a Black man, was shot and killed by Philadelphia Officer John Whiteside. The accusation: shoplifting. The *Philadelphia Inquirer* recounted what happened. Truman was chased into an alley by Whiteside, and when Truman asked a simple question—what had he done wrong?—Whiteside shot him. Whiteside was later convicted of manslaughter.

Since Truman's killing, a steady stream of Black people

have been killed by law enforcement, including over 1,300 since 2017, according to data from Statista, a digital insights company. Too many Black families have lost too many of their sons, daughters, sisters, and brothers. This tragedy must stop.

THE FINAL WORD: We can change. Policing can change. It will take work, but it's possible.

If you see an unarmed Black man shot by police, resist the urge to think he should have complied. Remember history, critical thinking, and legitimate news sources. Also, remember history. Why do I say that?

This was the original statement released by the Minneapolis Police Department after George Floyd was murdered. I hope that there is transformational growth from his murder. When we fail to learn from history, it will repeat itself. It was a lie, designed to protect officers. Never forget this:

Man Dies After Medical Incident During Police Interaction

May 25, 2020 (MINNEAPOLIS) On Monday evening, shortly after 8:00 pm, officers from the Minneapolis Police Department responded to the 3700 block of Chicago Avenue South on a report of a forgery in progress. Officers were advised that the suspect was sitting on top of a blue car and appeared to be under the influence.

Two officers arrived and located the suspect, a male believed to be in his 40s, in his car. He was ordered to step from his car. After he got out, he physically resisted officers. Officers were able to get the suspect into handcuffs and noted he appeared to be suffering medical distress. Officers called for an ambulance. He was transported to Hennepin County Medical Center by ambulance where he died a short time later.

At no time were weapons of any type used by anyone involved in this incident.

The Minnesota Bureau of Criminal Apprehension has been called in to investigate this incident at the request of the Minneapolis Police Department.

No officers were injured in the incident.

Citations

- Alexander, M. (2010). *The New Jim Crow: Mass Incarceration in the Age of Colorblindness.*
- COPS Office. (2015). *Final Report of the President's Task Force on 21st Century Policing.* U.S. Department of Justice.
- DOJ. (2023). "Investigation of the Louisville Metro Police Department." U.S. Department of Justice.

- Du Bois, W. E. B. (1935). *Black Reconstruction in America*.
- Hadden, S. E. (2001). *Slave Patrols: Law and Violence in Virginia and the Carolinas*.
- Statista. (2023). "Number of Black People Killed by Police in the U.S. Since 2017."
- Weaver, A. (2023). "Corruption in East Cleveland Police Department." *The Plain Dealer*.

CHAPTER EIGHT:

STAY WOKE

The city where I live in Pennsylvania is progressive and full of good people. That doesn't mean we don't get our occasional extremists. Once, there was a peaceful protest in support of the Black Lives Matter movement at a park in town, and a small group of white men showed up wearing military gear and carrying automatic weapons. Most recently, right-wing groups, as they have around the country, have been attempting to infiltrate our local school boards. In places like Florida, these groups attempt to ban certain books, many of them about Black history. One of these groups came to my town and I saw literature from them railing against "wokeness." I don't speak for all Black people (that job doesn't pay enough), but I believe when many of us hear complaints about wokeness, we hear anti-Blackness. There's no question that the right-wing obsession with being woke is about suppressing Blackness. If you don't understand that (I'll clarify shortly).

When I heard about anti-wokeness possibly influencing our school board, I felt strongly it was time to say something. In February of 2023, I spoke to the board, and I started by saying how fear, ignorance and intimidation affects all of us.

"In our community, right now, we have individuals who have made it their business to use untruths to impact the way we see each other," I told the board. "Last week we had a group organize and pass out flyers of five candidates that are running for the school board that don't want you to talk about diversity, inclusion, LGBTQ issues. I don't think that's what this community is about...so my request of you is to not fear wokeness. I want you to be awake. I want you to see me. I want you to understand my humanity.

"And we have some individuals that want us to have our heads in the sand...So my request of you is to really understand the history of our country, the beauty and the ugliness, all of it together. I prefer that we do not walk around blinded and misinformed and ignorant. I promise you if we do, history will repeat itself...the playbook is always the same. George Wallace of Alabama picked up the same playbook, and some folks are reusing that same playbook today. Do not allow it to happen here in our community."

A few weeks after I spoke to the school board, I was contacted by a man who identified himself as Black, and he said how watching me speak to the board had impacted him. He was 50 years old and felt that for years he'd put his Blackness on hold. But that was going to stop. I cried on that call with him, and it reminded me of how important it is to speak up, to fight the people who want to stifle or destroy Blackness. Also, you never know who's watching. You never know who you're going to impact.

—

Nikki Haley, the former South Carolina governor, said in 2023 that "wokeness is a virus more dangerous than any pandemic, hands down." She apparently forgot the coronavirus pandemic killed over one million Americans (CDC, 2023).

"We must fight 'the woke' in our schools. We must fight 'the woke' in our businesses. We must fight 'the woke' in government agencies," DeSantis said at a campaign event in 2023. "We can never, ever surrender to woke ideology. And I'll tell you this, the state of Florida is where woke goes to die. (The New York Times, 2023)"

DeSantis is more than talk. He signed into law the "Stop WOKE" Act. At its core, it chills free speech, and attempts to stop people from talking about race. It does this by using severe penalties, threats of firing teachers, and yanking funding from state schools (Florida Department of Education, 2022). What makes the act so pernicious is how it targets Black educators. It doesn't go after, say, the teaching of European history. Mainly, just Black history.

Black people have been using the word woke since at least the 1960s and maybe even decades earlier. Journalist Elijah Watson traced it back to one place in particular: "...It is fascinating to consider that woke originated in Harlem. For most of the 20th century, Harlem was the epicenter of Black culture. From the Harlem Renaissance to the Black Arts Movement, there's a reason why Harlem was once referred to as America's Black Capital. So, it's not far-fetched to believe woke was birthed here because countless Black people discovered themselves and one another here. They were awakened here. But it's also beautiful to think that woke was its own community colloquialism (Watson, 2021). That it wasn't beatnik slang, jazz slang, or jive slang, but Harlem slang — a word said on certain blocks by certain people throughout the neighborhood, now said by people across the world. For better or worse."

The word was introduced to a more modern audience in 2008 with Erykah Badu's song "Master Teacher" (featuring spoken word by Georgia Anne Muldrow). The phrase she specifically introduced was "stay woke" (Muldrow & Badu, 2008).

The white backlash to the word started soon after the Black Lives Matter movement began. Black protestors told each other to stay woke around the police. In this way, history repeated itself. Author and journalist Michael Harriot told the Legal Defense Fund for a story it did on wokeness: "When people during the civil rights movement began saying 'Black power,' all of a sudden it became a term that people equated with communism and anti-white sentiment—and then it eventually gave birth to 'white power.' The '1619 Project' has become an insult. 'Black Lives Matter' became an 'anti-white sentiment' that was banned in school and spawned 'all lives matter' and 'blue lives matter'" (Harriot, 2022).

The problem isn't just DeSantis. It's that his actions in Florida are a blueprint for other red state governors who have happily followed his lead. The whole performative anti-woke movement even reached Capitol Hill. In March of 2023, a Democratic Congressman from Rhode Island,

THE FINAL WORD: The use of "woke" as a negative is a way of dividing all of us, and distracting from significant, real issues that impact our lives.

All of this is the reason I spoke to the school board and why I'll fight about this issue. Because, at its core, anti-wokeness is anti-Blackness. So, stay woke.

Citations

- Centers for Disease Control and Prevention (CDC). (2023). "COVID-19 Death Data."
- Florida Department of Education. (2022). *Overview of the Stop WOKE Act.*
- Harriot, M. (2022). "The Weaponization of Woke." Legal Defense Fund.
- Muldrow, G. A., & Badu, E. (2008). *Master Teacher* [Song]. New Amerykah Part One.
- The New York Times. (2023). "DeSantis's Anti-Woke Agenda and Its Implications."
- Watson, E. (2021). "Tracing the Roots of Woke." *The Undefeated.*
- Whitehouse, S. (2023). Congressional Press Briefing. Rhode Island Capitol.

CHAPTER NINE

MY DAD, THE BOND, AND THE MYTH OF SCARCITY

It was October of 2019, when I met a senior executive for a major investment firm, following a session I led on unconscious bias at his company. He approached me after the session and explained it was nothing like he expected. He shared that three people he knew who attended similar training said their sessions were all about bashing white men.

I said, "No, that's not my approach." We kept talking and the conversation was friendly and honest. He asked if it was okay to stay in contact. He wanted me to facilitate a community wide event he was coordinating that would last five days: the first with school leaders; the second with faith-based leaders; the third with first responders; the fourth with economic leaders; and the last day would happen at a Black-owned farm where all of the groups would come together. There, everyone would discuss their experiences and focus on how to create a sense of togetherness and belonging in their communities and beyond.

It was all supposed to come together just some months after me and that executive met, but then, my father died in May of 2020. I told him the session would have to be postponed, and he was deeply sympathetic and offered his condolences. He then told me a personal story. He'd experienced his father passing and had struggled with that loss for years. One day he ran into this shaman who said to him: Why are you running from the pain? The shaman asked him to accept the pain because it's the bond between him and his father. Those words hit me hard.

It left me welcoming the grief, pain, and mourning. It was a gift to have my father. He and I had a close relationship, and he is always with me. Occasionally, I turn toward the waves of emotion and allow them to wash over me. To this day, I'm still learning the new language between my father and me.

So, let's recap. One man attends mandatory unconscious bias training. He enters it believing that it's going to suck—it's just more white male bashing. I disrupt that framing. He approaches me being open and vulnerable. After a few months, my father passes because of complications related to COVID. This guy is one of the first people I speak with, and he offers me the reframing and comfort I need. This is a perfect example of humans just being human with each other and how we can cross the chasms, often artificial ones, between us.

Meeting that executive, and how we connected on such a human level, reminded me of a common theme of when I talk to companies and individuals who are (mainly) white: when fear is overcome, we make connections. Fear is among the most corrosive of emotions. Fear of difference, fear of the other. Fear can run amok and cause otherwise brilliant people to behave in ways they never normally would. I see that once I start talking to people, reaching them, like I did with that executive, showing them that fear is a destructive monster that can be corralled. That's when the real conversations begin. Once fear is destroyed, I can almost always reach people. When that moment happens, we all become human, and the differences that should be minor, become minor again.

There's a common theme in some of the right-wing media and politics I see that does the opposite of quell fear. There's this belief that white people are now the oppressed. This is not a small thing or imagined; it is so remarkably real. It's part of the trope of the great replacement theory that former Fox host Tucker Carlson spoke about on his shows to millions of people before he was fired in 2023 (Southern Poverty Law Center, 2023). The affirmative action cases before the Supreme Court quite literally say that white people are entitled to spots at Ivy League schools because they just are.

In many ways, all of this is the opposite of what happened between me and that executive, and instead there was an example of a variation of an economic principle called the **myth of scarcity**.

The myth of scarcity has its roots in classical economics, particularly the work of Thomas Malthus. Malthus addressed the perils of population growth and believed there'd be so many people we would outgrow food production (Malthus, An Essay on the Principle of Populations, 1798). This idea became known as the "Malthusian trap," and it was used to justify everything from colonialism to eugenics. The myth of scarcity was further reinforced by the development of neoclassical economics in the late 19th and early 20th centuries. Neoclassical economists, such as Alfred Marshall and

William Stanley Jevons, emphasized the importance of competition and market efficiency. They argued that resources were scarce because they were finite, and that the only way to allocate them efficiently was through the price mechanism.

The myth has had a profound impact on economic and social policy over the past century. It has been used to justify a wide range of policies, including austerity, privatization, and deregulation. It has also been used to justify economic systems that are based on competition and market efficiency, such as capitalism. One of its primary implications is that it creates a zero-sum mentality. This mentality assumes that there is a fixed amount of resources to go around, and that any gains made by one person or group must necessarily come at the expense of another. This creates a sense of competition and conflict, which can lead to social and economic problems. Mainly, the concept is dead wrong because it becomes an engine for selfishness and greed.

I would argue that we're also seeing this myth of scarcity being applied to race. It's the idea that other people are getting things that should be coming to you. And by "other people," it mainly means Black people and immigrants. And by you, it usually means white people. The myth of scarcity in terms of race has shown itself in several ways:

1. The portrayal of Black people as "welfare queens" in political discourse, which perpetuates the myth that they are taking resources away from others (Gilliam, *Farther to Go: Readings and Cases in African-American Politics*, 1994).

2. The portrayal of immigrants as "job stealers" in media, which perpetuates the myth that there is a limited number of jobs to go around (Pew Research Center, 2021).

3. The depiction of Indigenous peoples as "savages" in media, which perpetuates the myth that their land and resources are up for grabs (Dunbar-Ortiz, *An Indigenous Peoples' History of the United States*, 2014).

4. The portrayal of Asian Americans as "model minorities," which perpetuates the myth that some groups are more deserving of resources than others (Chou & Feagin, *The Myth of the Model Minority*, 2016).

5. The exclusion of Black and brown communities from access to necessities such as clean water and healthcare, which perpetuates the myth that some communities are not worthy of resources (Flint Water Crisis, Michigan Civil Rights Commission, 2017).

What I see a great deal of today are politicians on the right, as well as the media, pushing us to fight each other by spreading messages that one group is stealing from the other. They pit us against each other. It's a variation of what President Lyndon Johnson once said:

"If you can convince the lowest white man he's better than the best colored man, he won't notice you're picking his pocket. Hell, give him somebody to look down on, and he'll empty his pockets for you" (Caro, *The Years of Lyndon Johnson: Master of the Senate*, 2002).

What I also see are examples of what that executive and I experienced. Once we just talked, and connected, all the external voices that try to divide us melted away. We were just two people, talking about loss, care, and father and son love. We were people. That's all.

Citations

- Caro, R. (2002). *The Years of Lyndon Johnson: Master of the Senate*. Vintage Books.
- Chou, R. S., & Feagin, J. R. (2016). *The Myth of the Model Minority: Asian Americans Facing Racism*. Routledge.
- Dunbar-Ortiz, R. (2014). *An Indigenous Peoples' History of the United States*. Beacon Press.

- Gilliam, F. D. (1994). *Farther to Go: Readings and Cases in African-American Politics*. Harcourt Brace College.
- Malthus, T. (1798). *An Essay on the Principle of Population*. J. Johnson.
- Michigan Civil Rights Commission. (2017). *Report on the Flint Water Crisis*.
- Pew Research Center. (2021). *Attitudes Toward Immigrants and Jobs*.
- Southern Poverty Law Center. (2023). *Tracking the Spread of the Great Replacement Theory*.

CHAPTER TEN

MENTAL WEALTH

Growing up, whenever I'd get angry, my mom would always ask several questions. "Just let me know how long you're going to be upset," she'd say. "One hour? Two? Is this one of those all day upset things? Just know," she'd remind me, "that if you're upset, you give up control and power."

My dad was completely different. He emphasized defending yourself. If someone says something that's sideways—hit them. I grew up appreciating aggression, especially in York, Pennsylvania, where I attended a predominantly white daycare and elementary school.

Since my parents were extremely active in civil rights, I knew that it was always possible some kid or parent, who maybe disliked Black people, would come after me either verbally or physically. My dad always said: "Defend yourself with words but also physically if you need to." My mom wasn't cool with that at all.

When I had my own sons, I have to say, my mom's strategy won. I always want them to defend themselves, but I tell them that physical violence should only be used as a last resort. Unfortunately, I was forced to put this philosophy to the test. My youngest son was bullied in middle school by five kids for about three months. I am so proud of how he handled it. He used words to try and deflate it, not violence. He was the bigger person.

I told my son I would help him, but I struggled with this situation. My father's voice was running amuck in my head. My initial reaction was to show up at five houses and deal with it directly. I did visit with the parents of one of the bullies, and the family responded well. I was prepared to escalate the situation and visit the remaining four families, but then I heard my mom's voice in my head and realized doing that wouldn't be good for anyone. I engaged the middle school principal to connect with the parents of the bullies and the bullies themselves. I facilitated a workshop around bias and trauma with all of the adults at the middle school.

But it was not an easy thing. We got him mental health therapy and even got him involved in yoga. The idea was to release it all, from not just his mind but also his body. He doesn't naturally trust people, but he's also been working through that. Witnessing his growth through this process is remarkable. I worked on myself as well. I attended an eight-week Mindfulness Based Stress Release (MBSR) session. It teaches people how to better deal with stress and anxiety (American Psychological Association, 2020). It was amazing. I also helped facilitate an unconscious bias session for all the adults at this middle school. There were things that happened in the classroom that the adults failed to catch. They failed to catch it because they didn't *see* my little brown kid in their classroom.

So, what does this have to do with mental health? Imagine the loving conversations my father had with me. He was trying to help me survive in a world he knew was hostile to people who looked like us. Despite his best intentions, some aspects of those conversations turned into toxic masculinity for me. I'm still navigating the learning edges of that. As a result, I wasn't fully equipped to deal with the care that my son needed, which an amazing therapist provided.

2022, Seven years later, I found myself facilitating a conversation with twenty Black men at another event in Maryland. The discussion was about reimagining mental health. At the end of the two-hours session, none of us want to leave the conversations we had started. My main message is that I want Black people to think about their mental health. There's an author named Jason Wilson who wrote the book *Cry Like a Man: Fighting for Freedom from Emotional Incarceration*.

"Although I've experienced many losses and tragedies in my life," Wilson writes, "it was the absence and condemning words of my father that caused the most trauma—forming a deficit mentality and sentencing me to years in emotional incarceration" (Wilson, 2019).

A *Publisher's Weekly* review notes: "He calls the lasting hurt caused by these early experiences 'father wounds.' He believes that generational trauma is compounded for boys and men because they are granted few outlets for processing it. 'The greatest challenge I believe males of all ages are facing today is that they fear being transparent will compromise their manliness,' Wilson says. *Cry Like a Man* recounts Wilson›s journey toward healing his wounds and clears a path for other men who want to heal their own wounds and break free from misconstrued masculinity."

For me, on many occasions, I accepted trauma as cultural and walked around carrying unnecessary weight. I refuse to carry it anymore. I have a therapist. I have a group of brothers that hold me accountable. And I have my crew where I just shoot the shit. I am also grateful for the foundational work that Omega Psi Phi has imparted me with. Our fraternity's four cardinal principles— Manhood, Scholarship, Perseverance and Uplift—were what got me through college and are the muscle memory my brain needs to confront the issues a Black husband, father and business owner faces daily.

●━━●

What's also clear is that mental health issues aren't solely about parent and child relationships. Racism also causes trauma, mental health crises and anxieties. Don't take my word for it. There is science that supports this.

A study in the *Journal of Affective Disorders* in June of 2023 showed that "racial discrimination was associated with increased odds for 12-month and lifetime anxiety disorders, agoraphobia (AG - Agoraphobia is an anxiety disorder where a person believes their environment is unsafe and there's no easy way to escape), and panic disorder (PD) and lifetime social anxiety disorder (SAD) among men. Regarding 12-month disorders among women, racial discrimination was associated with increased odds for any anxiety disorder, PTSD, SAD, and PD. With respect to lifetime disorders among women, racial discrimination was associated with increased odds for any anxiety disorder, PTSD, generalized anxiety disorder, SAD, and PD" (Journal of Affective Disorders, 2023).

"Racial discrimination is a social stressor that threatens the lives and livelihoods of African Americans," the report states. "It demeans and devalues minoritized individuals and subjects them to social and economic disadvantage. In addition to limiting access to needed material and social resources, experiencing and coping with discrimination is emotionally and cognitively taxing and initiates a stress response...even the anticipation of prejudice or discrimination is a stressor with physiological consequences. Thus, prolonged and repeated experiences of discrimination and the anticipation of these experiences can contribute to the physiological dysregulation that subsequently leads to multiple physical, cognitive and mental ailments. Racial discrimination may be particularly salient for anxiety disorders among African Americans because it threatens a person's sense of self-worth and social belonging, which can manifest generally as excessive fear and anxiety, two emotional and cognitive hallmarks of anxiety disorders, respectively."

These issues impact every aspect of Black life, and we see societal examples of how Black mental health is often neglected or ignored. One such instance is in the military. In 2022, a new report surfaced from an internal Veterans

Affairs report from 2017 that showed Black veterans were denied benefits for PTSD more than white ones (Center for Investigative Reporting, 2022).

Black veterans, the report stated, "were denied disability benefits for PTSD 57 percent of the time, as opposed to 43 percent for white veterans between the years 2011-2016." Just imagine the impact the lack of support for the Black military vets has had on those service persons, their families, and communities. The systemic issues across the board, and not just in the military, have been severe and will continue to have an impact for generations.

What I hope is that people like my son, Ivan, with his open heart and mind, even in the face of bullies, and the strategies he's learned to armor his mental health, can be an example for others. For all others.

Citations:

- American Psychological Association. (2020). *Mindfulness-Based Stress Reduction (MBSR)*.
- Center for Investigative Reporting. (2022). *Black Veterans and PTSD Benefits*.
- Journal of Affective Disorders. (2023). *Racial Discrimination and Mental Health Disorders in African Americans*.
- Wilson, J. (2019). *Cry Like a Man: Fighting for Freedom from Emotional Incarceration*.

CHAPTER ELEVEN

THE KAEPERNICK FACTOR

Everything about my youth was connected to being an athlete. I played both football and ran track. Both were about winning every moment and with football, especially, it was also about being physical. What I also know to be true is excelling in both enhanced my drive to win.

I was driven to understand what would make me better. What drills, what speed techniques, what overall techniques, and overall strategies would achieve that. I often asked myself these questions. What should I learn and study? This broke down into two different layers of competition. There was the internal competition with myself: Did I get the reps in on the track? Was I in the weight room enough? What's my personal best on the track?

There was also the external competition. In high school, I often thought about where I ranked on the team, county, state and nationally. What would running on the collegiate level look like?

Like other dedicated athletes, in high school I didn't socialize as much as my non-athlete counterparts, because so much time was required for sports. Please don't get it too twisted. There were a few clubs in the DMV (District of Columbia, Maryland and Virginia area) that I went to with some close friends. However, mostly, so much of my high school life was working out. I skipped some family or school events because I needed to get a workout in. This is the life of many athletes.

I loved sports and what it did for me, but some of that joy and accomplishment came with a price. Some of my friendships weren't as nurtured as they should have been. I was too focused on being great at track. At times, I was too focused solely on myself.

That changed my senior year of college. I pledged Omega Psi Phi and when you connect with your line brothers it can never be just about you. Being a Bruh reinforced what it means to be part of a team. It validated the importance of service for the collective good. Also, as I entered the workforce, and I began seeing some of the backbiting and sabotage, being in a fraternity also schooled me on how to be above it. Hurting people to advance myself was never in my DNA. However, striving to be number one can have unintended consequences. Being conscious of the impact we have on others is critical.

What the fraternity taught me wasn't just perseverance. It was how the process, at times, could be a unifier. Similarly football was unifier allowing me and my teammate to bond for a common purpose. Sports can also be a vehicle for peaceful, strong protest. The opportunity to have access in various sports and perform with excellence. Opportunities to dispel harmful normative beliefs about people. It may not always seem like it, but sports have been one of the largest mechanisms for change. Jesse Owens won four gold medals in the 1936 Munich Olympics with Hitler watching from the stands, disproving the myth of Aryan superiority (PBS, 2008). Tommie Smith and John Carlos raising their fist at the 1968 Olympics in Mexico raised awareness to the plight of Black Americans fighting racism and oppression in the United States (Smith, 2007).

Black athletes have long used their platforms to speak out against racial injustice and discrimination. We were often excluded from mainstream leagues and teams, forced to compete in segregated leagues and events that offered fewer resources and opportunities. Despite those challenges, however, athletes used their skills and talents to excel in their sports and to challenge the status quo. There are numerous examples of this including the Negro Leagues, as they were called, providing a platform for players to showcase their talents and to challenge the racist assumptions that had long kept them out of the mainstream.

Black baseball players such as Jackie Robinson and Satchel Paige became legends in the Negro Leagues. Robinson would go on to change the course of baseball and societal history by breaking the color barrier in Major League Baseball in 1947 and using his platform to speak out against racism and discrimination throughout his career and life (Robinson, 1972).

In the 1960s and 1970s, Black athletes became increasingly involved in the civil rights movement and used their platforms to support the cause of racial justice and equality. Muhammad Ali refused to be drafted into the Vietnam War, citing his opposition to the war and his belief in nonviolent protest (Remnick, 1998). He was stripped of his boxing titles and faced significant backlash from the media and the government, but he remained steadfast in his commitment to his beliefs and his activism.

Now, after being hated then, he is one of the most beloved Americans in history.

There are few better examples of using the power of sports for positive societal change than Colin Kaepernick.

—

Kaepernick, a former NFL quarterback, has become a symbol of freedom and justice for his courageous decision to kneel during the national anthem in protest against racial injustice and police brutality. He has been called a freedom fighter because he used his platform as a professional athlete to speak out against systemic racism and to demand accountability and change.

Kaepernick's protest began in 2016 when he was playing for the San Francisco 49ers. Initially, during the pre-game national anthem of a preseason game, he took a seat on the bench. Eventually, he started to kneel during the anthem, a gesture he adopted after consulting with former Green Beret Nate Boyer, who suggested it as a respectful form of protest (*New York Times, 2016*). Kaepernick explained that he was protesting the treatment of African Americans and other people of color by law enforcement, and that he would continue to do so until there was significant progress towards racial equality.

Kaepernick's decision to kneel during the national

anthem started a debate that engulfed the entire nation, with many people supporting his right to peaceful protest and others condemning him as unpatriotic. Some NFL players and other athletes followed his lead, taking a knee during the anthem to show solidarity with his cause. However, some others accused him of disrespecting the flag and the military. Of course, that was a lie. Kaepernick himself stated repeatedly and explicitly his purpose. "I am not protesting the anthem or the nation," Kaepernick told the *Sporting News*, "I'm protesting organized brutality. To me, this is much bigger than football and it would be selfish to look the other way. There are bodies in the street and people getting paid leave and getting away with murder" (Sporting News, 2016).

Despite the backlash, Kaepernick continued to use his platform to speak out against racism and police brutality. He donated $1 million to various organizations working towards social justice and led a campaign to raise awareness about police violence against Black and brown people. He also started the "Know Your Rights" camp, a youth campaign designed to educate young people about their legal rights and to empower them to act against social injustice.

Kaepernick's activism has had a significant impact on the national conversation about race and social justice. His protests drew attention to the fact that people of color are disproportionately targeted by police and are more likely to face violence and discrimination than their white counterparts. He also challenged the idea that patriotism requires blind loyalty to the government and its symbols, arguing that true patriotism means standing up for the rights of all Americans, including those who are marginalized and oppressed.

THE FINAL WORD: Despite his impact on the national conversation about race and social justice, Kaepernick has faced significant backlash and even personal attacks because of his activism. His activism challenged the narrative of what patriotism means. His actions align with the traditions of civil disobedience exemplified by leaders like Dr. Martin Luther King Jr. He was blacklisted by the NFL and has not played in a professional football game since the 2016 season, despite being a talented and experienced quarterback. He has also faced criticism from conservative politicians and media outlets, who have accused him of being anti-American and unpatriotic.

However, Kaepernick's supporters argue that his activism is a powerful example of what it means to be a true patriot. They argue that he is fighting for the principles that the United States was founded on equality, justice, and freedom and that he is using his platform to hold the government and law enforcement accountable for their actions. They also argue that his protest is a peaceful and nonviolent form of resistance, consistent with the tradition of civil disobedience and social movements in American history.

In essence, Kaepernick was impacted by those that came before him. Althea Gibson and Jackie Robinson and Jesse Owens and Ali all paved the way or gave him the blueprint. That is what made him great. That is what makes sports so powerful. All of these human understood the assignment regarding nonviolent protest and caring for their bodies. In what ways do you engage in nonviolent protest, transformational protest, while staying keenly aware of your body and capacity

The question remains: How will we continue to engage in meaningful protest and activism while caring for ourselves physically and emotionally? Kaepernick reminds us that action and resilience can coexist, paving the way for future athletes and activists to continue the fight for justice.

Citations

- PBS. (2008). *Jesse Owens and the 1936 Olympics.*
- Smith, T. (2007). *Silent Gesture: The Autobiography of Tommie Smith.*
- Robinson, J. (1972). *I Never Had It Made: An Autobiography of Jackie Robinson.*

- Remnick, D. (1998). *King of the World: Muhammad Ali and the Rise of an American Hero*.
- New York Times. (2016). *Colin Kaepernick Takes a Stand by Taking a Knee*.
- Sporting News. (2016). *Colin Kaepernick Explains Why He Kneels*.
- Know Your Rights Camp. (2023). *About Us*.

CHAPTER TWELVE

THE BLACK BOARDROOM

T*he writing below is from a healthcare professional at a major American hospital and this person is also a friend. I was given permission to use it for this book. This person wanted to remain anonymous. The words are powerful because while they are about working in the hospital system, which as we've already discussed can sometimes be dismissive, and even hostile, to people of color, this writing could apply to many different situations in* *business and corporate America. The question asked is: What if the boardroom was Black?*

What if you walked into a boardroom and everyone around you was Black? How would you feel? You've always wanted to work here because it's the best place for cancer care and your cancer experience as a young child made you passionate for this line of work. You respect your colleagues because they truly are the best at what they do. They are bright, innovative, daring, and resourceful. You are so proud of yourself for "making it."

Now, wouldn't it be nice if one Black person came to you and said: "I'm going to make sure you succeed here." I'm going to give you some tips on what to say, who to meet, what you should know and do to work your way up. I'm going to try to carve out a path for you here and make sure that you are well connected, informed, and involved in the large, important institutional priorities so that you are recognized and can advance because it will be hard for you if I don't. I'm going to make sure you go to the right conferences (expenses paid) and sign up for Toastmasters. Wouldn't that be nice! The room wouldn't look so scary. You wouldn't have to locate the one or two other white people in the room to feel comfortable.

Maybe you always thought that if you work hard, do your research, stay up to date on the most recent news related to your field, that your dedication would be acknowledged. But how can you compete? These folks have known each other for many years. They've attended each other's weddings and talk about their kids and even vacation together. They share dinner and drinks often after work and text each other when running late to meetings. It is very clear that you are an outsider. You quickly learn that to penetrate through friendship and connections with just "hard work" alone is a joke. You're not looking for pity or special treatment. Equal opportunities. Equal exposure.

As you wait for the meeting to begin, you hear conversations in the background about how to help a family member get a job at our hospital or who to speak with to get into that exclusive high school. The underground locomotion in full swing. You wish you knew how to get your daughter into the best kindergarten, except quickly learn that you don't know, what you don't know. The unfairness of it all weighs heavy but you're used to it and continue to do your best and are grateful that you're here.

End dream.

CHAPTER THIRTEEN

THE LURE

Like many fathers, across many generations, mine taught me how to fish. We fished everywhere: on streams, on a boat, on a river or pond. There's nothing like the flow of a river and watching your line dance around in the water until it gets that hit of a fish trying to escape with your bait. Then, you get to work. Let it run for a minute and pull that line to set the hook. Start reeling it in. Taking it off the hook is another process. It's all about cleaning and preparing the fish for consumption. I know for certain that my fried fish can stand up to anyone's.

My father enjoyed my fried fish. Primarily because he taught me everything I know about catching, cleaning and cooking fish. All of it comes from my relationship with him and my uncle Larry Brown taking me fishing with them as a child. How much time do we spend in our youth learning life lessons to pass on? I need to spend more time showing my sons what I learned so they can pass it on. Fishing and the art of cooking fish cannot stop with me. This is about the honorable legacies and tradition we should pass down. It is time to let the world slow down. A space and time where you can just be.

Please know I'm talking about fishing but also much more. I'm also talking about the love of self and know thy self. I know who I am as a Black man, and I learned from being obedient, watching, and listening. I need to make certain my sons love all of themselves as Black men navigating in this world. I need to make certain they are not led hook, line, and sinker by the wrong influences. They are the fishermen of their fate.

As I said, this isn't just about fishing. Fishing represents history and love and friendship. Fishing has played an important role in the lives of Black people for centuries, both as a means of subsistence, and as a source of cultural identity and resistance.

During the era of slavery, fishing was a critical source of food for enslaved Africans, who were often tasked with fishing for the slave holders. After the Civil War, fishing continued to be an important economic activity for many Black Americans, particularly those living in rural areas with limited employment opportunities (The Southern Foodways Alliance, 2020). Black fishermen faced several challenges including discrimination and segregation. In some Southern states, Black fishermen were denied access to certain fishing grounds or markets or were required to pay discriminatory fees or taxes. Despite these challenges, many Black fishing communities thrived and developed unique cultures and traditions around fishing.

In the Chesapeake Bay region, Black fishermen developed a distinctive style of fishing known as "oyster tonging," which involved using long-handled tongs to collect oysters from the Bay's shallow waters (Smithsonian National Museum of African American History and Culture, 2019). This method of fishing required a great deal of skill and physical strength and became an important part of the region's Black culture.

In other areas, such as the Gulf Coast, Black fishermen played a critical role in the development of the commercial fishing industry. They were often skilled at catching shrimp, crabs, and other shellfish, which were in high demand. Despite facing discrimination and other obstacles, many Black fishermen were able to build successful fishing businesses and provide for their families (Sturtevant, 2018).

In the mid-twentieth century, the Civil Rights movement brought new attention to issues of racial discrimination and segregation in the fishing industry. In 1964, the Civil Rights Act was passed, which outlawed discrimination based on race, color, religion, sex, or national origin (*U.S. Department of Labor, 2023*). This law helped open new opportunities for Black fishermen and other workers in the fishing industry.

Additionally, the increased visibility of Black communities in industries like fishing contributed to a broader understanding of their historical and cultural contributions. Scholars and cultural historians have increasingly recognized the importance of fishing as a practice that connects Black Americans to their ancestral traditions, both in Africa and in the Americas (*Blount, 2021*).

Fishing, for many, is a way to connect with nature and tradition. For Black Americans, it is also a thread that weaves through history, connecting the resilience and ingenuity of enslaved people with the vibrancy of Black culture today. I talk throughout this book about history and how history constantly impacts us today. Sometimes that history is defined and has sharp edges. In other moments, that history is a father and son in a boat, bonding with fishing as the catalyst, the way fathers and sons have done for a thousand years.

Fishing reminds us of the importance of slowing down, of taking time to reflect, and of cherishing the lessons passed down through generations. It reminds us that the traditions we inherit are not just about survival, but about identity, community, and love.

THE FINAL WORD: As we continue to navigate life's waters, let us remember that we are all fishermen of our fate. The lures we choose, the patience we exhibit, and the care we show for the catch all mirror how we approach life itself. What we leave behind—the knowledge, love, and traditions—is what shapes future generations. Let us ensure they inherit a world where the rivers flow freely, and the lines cast connect us all.

Citations

- Southern Foodways Alliance. (2020). *Fishing and Black Cultural History in the South*.
- Smithsonian National Museum of African American History and Culture. (2019). *Oyster Tonging: A Black Tradition in Chesapeake Bay*.
- Sturtevant, V. (2018). *Black Fishermen and the Gulf Coast Fishing Industry: A Cultural Legacy*.
- U.S. Department of Labor. (2023). *The Civil Rights Act of 1964 and Its Impact on Labor*.

- Blount, B. (2021). *Cultural Connections: Fishing and African American History.*

CHAPTER FOURTEEN

THIRTY WAYS TO IMPROVE RACE RELATIONS

T his chapter serves as a practical guide offering actionable strategies to enhance understanding and cooperation among different racial groups. Its primary purpose is to provide readers with concrete steps to foster inclusivity, promote equality, and build harmonious communities. By implementing these methods, individuals and organizations can contribute to reducing racial tensions and creating a more equitable society.

1. **Don't let fear rule**. There's a reason this one is first. It's foundational. Fear keeps us from reaching out, from understanding, and from developing connections (*DiAngelo, R. 2018, "White Fragility"*).

2. **Read**. Information—legitimate information, not propaganda—is the key to staying educated about what's happening in the country and world. Evaluate the content and context that shapes your worldview. Consider broadening the content you consume (*National Education Association, 2023*)

3. **Broaden your circle of friends**. Meet people outside of your race and culture. Get uncomfortable with people. Get to know people outside of your circle (*Putnam, R., 2000, "Bowling Alone"*).

4. **Educate yourself on the history and experiences of different racial groups**. This is key in expanding our cultural humility. Please note this is inviting us to be mindful of cultural difference. Be willing to hold space for the both/and. Honoring the dignity for all (*Kendi, I. X., 2019, How to Be an Antiracist"*)

5. **Speak out against racism and discrimination**. Speak out because these assaults to the soul are

an assault on our collective humanity. Whether it happens in the classroom or the workplace, at a local or international level, we all have a responsibility to our collective humanity *(Edelman, M., 2015, "The Measure of Our Success")*.

6. **Support diversity and inclusion in all areas of life**. This is important because it shows you understand what it means to have broad coalitions. Work through any issues of "othering" you may have where you isolate or attack people who don't look like you (*Crenshaw, K., 1989, "Demarginalizing the Intersection of Race and Sex"*).

7. **Seek out opportunities to learn from people with different cultural backgrounds.** There's so much to learn as a steward of this planet (*Smithsonian Institution, 2023*).

8. **Avoid making assumptions based on stereotypes or biases.** This one is vital. It can also be the most challenging if you've failed to unpack how your perspectives and values originated. If you haven't, your biases will remain hidden from you (*Banaji, M., & Greenwald, A., 2016, "Blindspot: Hidden Biases of Good People"*).

9. **Acknowledge and address the impact of historical injustices.** This is related to point No. 2. Knowing history helps you understand

the present. Systemic issues require action and accountability (*Coates, T.-N., 2014, "The Case for Reparations"*).

10. **Promote equal access to educational and employment opportunities**. This should be a basic right, and we should look to close educational gaps, including the digital divide (*Pew Research Center, 2022*).

11. **Encourage diverse representation** in media and other forms of entertainment. Consuming media from a diverse representation is essential (*USC Annenberg Inclusion Initiative, 2022*).

12. **Support businesses owned by people from different racial backgrounds.** Economic empowerment contributes to equitable growth (*Minority Business Development Agency, 2023*).

13. **Take responsibility for one's own biases and prejudices.** This is often tough for people to do, but it's truly necessary. Why do I believe what I believe? When did I learn certain things are important? How are these beliefs impacting my interaction with others? This is about owning what you believe and understand the source without blame, shame or guilt (*Brown, B., 2012, "Daring Greatly"*). It is also about reckoning with believes that need to be addressed.

14. **Encourage open and honest conversations about race**. One suggestion is to read a book called *Difficult Conversations: How to Discuss What Matters Most* by Douglas Stone. Be honest with yourself about what you don't know (*Stone, D., Patton, B., & Heen, S., 2010*).

15. **Support organizations that work towards racial justice and equality.** Consider volunteering your time in diverse communities (*Southern Poverty Law Center, 2023*).

16. **Foster empathy and understanding towards people of different races.** Remember that having empathy isn't simple. It requires us to appreciate someone else's perspective, suspend our judgment, recognize the emotion someone is feeling, and acknowledge that emotion. These are defined as the four parts of empathy, according to nursing scholar Theresa Wiseman (*Wiseman, T., 1996, "Four Attributes of Empathy"*).

17. **Encourage children to learn about and appreciate diversity.** One of the reasons why some of the initiatives to restrict the teaching of Black history are so dangerous is because it sends a message to young people that diversity isn't important. Children learn from our actions more than our words. Prioritize books and media that

show diversity, and model inclusive behavior (*American Psychological Association, 2023*). Be truly mindful of how we show up in the world. Who do we gravitate towards, and when does restriction/resistance show up?

18. **Challenge racist or discriminatory comments and behavior.** We've all heard horrible racial language and seen terrible behavior. Stop people dead in their tracks when you spot it (*DiAngelo, R. 2018, "White Fragility"*). This practice takes lots of reps to make it second nature. This might be the similar or the same as No. 5 and worthy of repeating.

19. **Encourage diverse representation in leadership positions**. Allow space for different perspectives. Also, foster innovation, and better connection with others (*Harvard Business Review, 2022*).

20. **Advocate for fair and unbiased policing practices**. Review of policies, practices, rules, and laws are critical. Policies and community engagement must reflect inclusive principles (*21st Century Policing Task Force, 2015*). Engage those impacted by negative interactions with law enforcement early and often. Make sure the rules of the game are not harmful to others. Hold people accountable to make sure everyone follows

the new inclusive rules.

21. **Support policies that address systemic racism**. Explore the history of why the policies were put in place to start with (*The Brookings Institution, 2023*). Know the history. Truth telling is freeing!

22. **Hold oneself accountable for one's own actions and words.** This will be a lifelong journey of learning and unlearning. Holding yourself accountable to create new habits is a lifelong practice. Self-reflection is a lifelong practice (*Covey, S. R., 1989, "The 7 Habits of Highly Effective People"*). This about changing behaviors in order to connect with the humanity of others.

23. **Advocate for affordable housing and equal access to resources**. This has been an issue for decades, if not centuries, and has always been at the forefront of civil rights activists. It's about equal access to resources and treating people like human beings. Fair housing policies are critical for addressing systemic inequities (*Urban Institute, 2023*).

24. **Support multicultural education in schools**. If in fact we are aspirational about life, liberty, and the pursuit of happiness, this is a must in our school system. Note: it doesn't say life, liberty, assimilation, and the loss of culture and identity.

Teaching diverse histories and cultures enriches everyone (*National Education Association, 2023*).

25. **Use social media to promote racial equality and justice.** Extremists and racists use social media for their goals; the rest of us need to utilize it to counter them. I invite you to be a keyboard disruptor of harmful narratives (*Pew Research Center, 2023*). I also invite you to occasionally leave cyberspace and go talk to an actual human being.

26. **Support and amplify the voices of people from marginalized racial groups.** The dominant voice can fill up a room, take up space (*Crenshaw, K., 1989, "Intersectionality"*). Do we have a listening ear for the non-dominant voice and perspectives? Make space!

27. **Promote cultural competency training for professionals**. To be extremely knowledgeable of other cultures is a big ask. I am asking to learn aspects of other cultures. There's so much to learn and explore. Professional training builds bridges and breaks down barriers (*American Psychological Association, 2023*).

28. **Advocate for equal representation in government and politics.** We're still far away from politics being diverse and truly representing the racial makeup of the country. Consider being

active and striving for more diverse representation on local boards, who's missing from the table. Diverse leadership ensures more equitable policies (*Congressional Black Caucus Foundation, 2022*).

29. **Foster a sense of belonging for immigrants and refugees**. If you're not Indigenous, you're standing on stolen land. Remember who has the actual true rights. Please consider in what ways you ensure people are welcomed into your communities. Secondly please understand what matters most to the indigenous tribes in your area (*National Immigration Forum, 2023*). Do you know your own history, what land are your people from? What is the story of your ancestors?

30. **Use literature, museums and the arts to promote understanding.** There are so many beautiful ways to learn about each other. Engage with diverse stories and cultural expressions (*National Endowment for the Arts, 2023*). Explore all these forms of engagement like opera, poetry, ballet, theater, music, dance, and spoke word. Include discussions about the natural environment. Global warming is a significant problem, and the land is a teacher as well.

THE FINAL WORD: One last journal request. Write what you would add to this list. This is by no means complete. I want you to think of this as a starting point and a tool to help you explore your own list. I also invite you to please share this with your community.

TRUTH AND RECONCILIATION

I started this book by telling you about my mom, Dorothy. I wanted to finish with telling you about my dad, Lionel. Like my mom, he was a hero, and like my mom, he was fearless. My dad, in fact, helped start a movement.

To tell the story of my dad, and how he impacted my life, and why what he and many others did during one of America's most tumultuous eras still matters today, we must start in the late 1960s with several years of civil unrest in York, Pennsylvania, where he grew up. Much of the nation was experiencing racial strife particularly following violent actions by police against the Black community. The same happened in York.

My father's entrance into the civil rights world started with CORE: the Congress of Racial Equality. It remains one of the least known, but powerful and morally fortified, civil rights organizations in history. CORE was inspired by Mahatma Gandhi and his belief in peaceful protest and civil disobedience. It was started in 1942 in Chicago by a group of Black and white students and was a key cog at the various picket lines and sit-ins that would spring up across the South. They also played a key role in the Freedom Rides, the Montgomery Bus Boycott and were close allies of Martin Luther King, Jr.

CORE was dedicated to the ideal that the fight against injustice needed to be an effort from both Black and white people; it, in fact, needed to be a coalition of all races, which is something my father also believed. Brian Purnell wrote in his book *Fighting Jim Crow in the County of Kings (2013)*: "CORE hoped to create an interracial, nonviolent army that would end racial segregation in America with campaigns that employed what Gandhi called *satyagraha*, which translates as 'soul force' or 'truth force.' CORE founders believed that local chapters' public displays of interracial solidarity and disciplined use of nonviolence would transform America into a truly colorblind democratic society."

CORE's vision would shift following a series of horrific murders and bombings throughout the South. In 1964, police stopped CORE members James Chaney, Andrew Goodman, and Michael Schwerner (Goodman and Schwemer were white, Chaney was Black) for speeding in June of 1964. The three men were arrested, put into a county jail, and then released, eventually escorted to the edge of town by the police. About a month later, their bodies were found, and each had been shot and murdered. Nineteen men were later indicted on federal charges with seven convicted for civil rights violations. Unbelievably (or believably) none of the accused killers served a sentence of more than six years in prison. Decades later a former Klan leader named Edgar Ray Killen was convicted on three counts of manslaughter and sentenced to sixty years in prison.

Those murders, and the assassination of King, left some CORE members disenchanted with the idea of Blacks and whites working together. CORE would change, but my father remained committed to a multi-racial force to fight white nationalism. That's where the York Charrette story comes in.

It begins in the fall of 1969 when my dad, the director of Community Organization at York's Community

Progress Council, met William L. Riddick at a charrette, Riddick was leading at Shaw University in Raleigh, North Carolina. The charrette movement was described then by *Time* magazine as a type of civic group therapy and included a diverse membership. As the *York Daily Record* wrote in April of 2020: "The York Charrette targeted racially based discriminatory practices that had plagued York County for decades – and that had sparked unrest in the previous two summers. Affordable housing, access to health care and public transportation, economic opportunity inequities and the dogs used by police disproportionately against blacks headed the long list of issues on the table as the community converged at what is today known as The Bond."

The members would meet several times a day with one report from the event's health committee placing the opening-day attendance at 350, mostly white and mostly middle class. That number would top 500 some days. The "color scheme" as the *York Daily Record* noted, changed from white on Sunday to mostly Black on Wednesday.

"By Saturday and Sunday, we had about a 50-50 audience, old and young, Black and white," the report stated. The report added that hundreds of York's citizens participated and created several ideas that were commissioned. "It worked," his report stated. "Things really happened."

The report also stated: "Of course, (the) Charrette didn't solve all of York's problems, and wasn't expected to, but it did make a dent in the armor and for York that is saying a great deal."

"That multi-day dialogue came after a second summer of rioting on York's streets and recent violence at William Penn Senior High School," the York newspaper wrote. "No rioting occurred the summer after the spring 1970 event, which some credit to the Charrette process in which all of York's communities came together. Bailey played a big role in the forum, serving as Charrette Executive Committee chairman."

The charrette was like so many things about race in America: it was frustrating, full of love, full of caution but, mostly, it was full of hope. My dad helped start something in York and while it wasn't perfect, it was an example of how when fear is mitigated, and understanding is emphasized, we can truly understand one another.

My father died from COVID on May 4, 2020, in Maryland, where he'd spent much of his life. I was asked once during a podcast a tough question. Did I blame anyone for my father's death, particularly the staff *at the nursing home where he caught the virus?* I understand why some people might blame the staff, but it wasn't how I felt. Bluntly, my feelings are layered. When my father first tested positive, I could have wondered, or even blamed, the nursing home director for not enacting stricter measures, like temperature checks or mandatory mask usage, much sooner. There were facilities like the one my father was in that had either no cases or just one. ABC News did a story in May of 2020 about how the caregivers at one facility moved into the building where they worked for over 60 days to better protect the residents. There were no cases of COVID at that facility. If I wanted to blame someone, I might ask questions about why the staff at my father's facility didn't do something like that.

I tell this story because if I find it in my heart to not blame anyone, or anything, for my father's death while in a nursing home, others can find grace in theirs to not hate someone because of the color of their skin or other differences. Please note that I am fully aware the disproportionate death rates amongst black and brown bodies during COVID 19 pandemic.

The COVID-19 pandemic disproportionately affected Black and brown communities, with systemic disparities in healthcare access playing a significant role. According to the Centers for Disease Control and Prevention (CDC, 2021), Black Americans experienced hospitalization rates approximately 2.5 times higher than their white counterparts, underscoring structural inequities. My father's passing was deeply personal yet emblematic of these broader systemic failures.

As I reflect on his legacy, I am reminded of the teachings of Nelson Mandela, who once said, "Resentment is like drinking poison and then hoping it will kill your enemies" (*Long Walk to Freedom*, 1994). This perspective helped me channel grief into action and grace, resisting the urge to lay blame without context.

My father's death was traumatic but more important was his impact on my life, my family's life, which is almost impossible to measure. Or forget. His impact on the York community is also something that won't be forgotten. About fifteen years before his death, a man named Brett Greiman and some student assistants at the Bradley Academy for the Visual Arts composed a series of painted murals of 20th and early 21st century civil rights heroes in York. My father is featured on one of them. Greiman said the art was a monument to people who worked for peace and civil justice. That was my dad. That's me now. It can be you, too.

●━●

I started this book with a question: What is your legacy? Hopefully, I helped you find some answers to that question.

Throughout this book, I have shared stories of courage, pain, and hope, all with one goal: to inspire truth-telling and reconciliation in a divided world. These pages have been a journey—one that began with understanding my mother's unwavering belief in service and continued through deeply personal stories, historical insights, and moments of connection.

As my mother taught me, our legacy is defined not by what we accumulate but by what we leave behind for others. Her wisdom has been the compass guiding me through life, and it is her belief in the power of connection that I want to leave with you. Reconciliation begins with truth—acknowledging our shared history, no matter how painful, and using that knowledge to forge a path forward.

This journey has been both cathartic and challenging. Writing this book required me to confront my own fears and embrace vulnerability in sharing my truths. There were moments of deep sorrow as I revisited personal and collective pain. But there were also moments of hope and joy—witnessing the resilience of those who came before me and the potential for change in the hearts of those willing to listen.

One story that stands out is the gathering I hosted with my neighbors, where we reflected on what it means to live in a beloved community. Their words—about celebrating diversity, supporting one another, and fostering belonging—are etched in my memory. That conversation reminded me that reconciliation is not a grand, abstract idea; it begins in our living rooms, our schools, and our workplaces. It is rooted in small, everyday acts of kindness and understanding.

So, where do we go from here? How do we carry the lessons of this book into our own lives? I believe the first step is reflection. What is your legacy? How will you contribute to truth and reconciliation in your community? These questions are not meant to be a burden but to inspire. They are an invitation to join a collective.

I want to share a moment that occurred on a webinar with Joseph Marshall III, an elder from the Lakota tribe. It was during the height of the pandemic in 2020 and millions of people were home, in many cases isolated, and they were taking hard looks at themselves and not always liking what they saw. I asked him what the best way for people to deal with that phenomenon was. He relayed a story about "Iktomi" that's relevant even now, maybe *especially* now:

A man walks by a pond. The water is calm and when he peers into it, it's like looking into a mirror. He sees his reflection and likes what he sees. Then he leaves. He returns to the same pond on another day and it's windy and there are ripples in the pond. This time, when he looks into the water, his image is distorted. The man gets irritated that he can't see his face clearly and angrily walks away. On another day, he returns to the pond, it's raining, and the water moves chaotically, and his image isn't fixed, bouncing with the waves, and he gets even angrier than the day before.

A rabbit sits off to the side, watching every encounter of the man with the pond, and the rabbit laughed.

"What are you laughing at?" the man asked the rabbit.

"I'm laughing at you," the rabbit says. "You're upset, and the only thing that's changed is exterior to who you are. The only thing that's been different each time are things out of your control."

As we move forward in our lives, we often see distorted pictures of ourselves, sometimes caused by the media we consume that pushes division, or even because of some issues within ourselves. We must be careful that not only do we fail to recognize exactly who we are as that pond shifts from calm to stormy, but also not lose compassion for our fellow human beings. "If you do not know who you are, then it does not matter what you believe" (Joseph Marshall III).

Empathy, as defined by scholar Theresa Wiseman (1996), involves four key attributes: recognizing others' perspectives, suspending judgment, communicating understanding, and being emotionally present. These principles form the foundation of reconciliation. Truth-telling, as modeled in South Africa's post-apartheid Truth and Reconciliation Commission, is not just about acknowledging historical wrongs but about healing through shared humanity (*Tutu, D., 1999, "No Future Without Forgiveness"*). Empathy is connecting by way of hurt and/or harm. Compassion is about our collective healing.

The second item on that list—suspending judgment—can seem impossible, and it is difficult. Yet, it must be done if true progress is to be made. We can make space for empathy and compassion.

It may seem impossible now, but the reset I mentioned earlier can happen. In your life and in our society. It must. It will.

▬

Lastly, here's a story about hope, promise, and the future—a reminder that all of us, especially Black people, are filled with limitless potential. Despite how difficult things may seem, the future remains bright. This story begins somewhat unusually: with a handful of dirt.

Hope is more than optimism; it is a commitment to action despite uncertainty. As Lonnie Bunch, Secretary of the Smithsonian Institution, observed during the founding of the National Museum of African American History and Culture, "We are all shaped by the resilience and resistance of those who came before us" (*Smithsonian*

Magazine, 2016). The gift of dirt from Africa symbolizes the grounding force of history—reminding us that our identities are deeply rooted in our ancestors' resilience. It was a moving moment for me. I think we sometimes forget that, in some ways, we all come from land and for Black people in America, our lives, our connection to the planet, is through that dirt in Africa.

As I hold dirt in my hands, I am reminded of Dr. Maya Angelou's words: "I come as one, but I stand as ten thousand" (*On the Pulse of Morning*, 1993). This dirt represents not only the past but the limitless possibilities of the future. It signifies respect for my ancestors and hope for my descendants, an invitation to all of us to contribute to a collective reset of our humanity.

One of the reasons why it was illegal to teach slaves to read, was that slave owners didn't want Black people to know about their past or future. If you have no grounding in the past, and no hope, which is the future, you are lost. A people with no history, no holding of dirt, is inert.

Not long after that moment watching the interview, I found myself holding dirt in my own hands. I'm going to pass it down to my descendants. Why? As a child, I grew up in a house in York, Pennsylvania. We moved to Suitland, Maryland when I was around seven years old, and we lived in the Surrey Square Apartments from age seven to 17. After college, I lived in other apartment buildings before purchasing my first home in Teaneck, New Jersey.

That was decades ago. In 2023, my wife and I purchased a second home. I'm holding dirt in my own hands. This soil is from a state that has had some of the highest number of enslaved Americans. Yet, I know I want to pass it down to my descendants. I'm only sharing this because it's about my ancestors and descendants.

This dirt isn't just dirt. It represents respect for the past and hope for the future. There is always hope. Please consider connecting your hope to unimaginable possibilities!

So, where do we go from here? How do we carry the lessons of this book into our own lives? I believe the first step is reflection. What is your legacy? How will you contribute to truth and reconciliation in your community? These questions are not meant to burden but to inspire. They are an invitation to join a collective. What's the reset on our humanity?

FINAL REFLECTION: Take a moment to journal your thoughts. What will you pass on? How will you embody reconciliation in your actions? This is not merely an individual endeavor but a collective call to action. Together, we can transform history's distortions into clarity, its wounds into healing, and its divisions into unity.

ACKNOWLEDGMENTS

First and foremost, I want to thank Barto, Helen, Waymon and Eartha (my grandparents), Dorothy and Lionel Bailey, Janine, Kalil and Ivan Bailey, My sister Robbin Brittingham, and the rest of the tribe.

I also want to thank my lifelong connections from District Heights Boys and Girls Club, Suitland High School, and Fairleigh Dickinson University. All the bruhz from Omega Psi Phi Fraternity, specifically the bruhz from Tau Mu chapter (Fairleigh Dickinson University) and Nu Beta Beta (Teaneck, NJ). Thank you to Lee McDonald, Darren Burton, Kevin Grayson, Resmaa Menakem, Russell Ledet, Ken Hardy, and Bob Hluchy.

Those other aunts: Aunt Mae Pica, Aunt Tressie Griffin, Aunt Hildagarde Sissy Connor, and others who assisted with paving the way.

Thank you to Dr. Jacqueline Smalls Goodnight, Ms. Hilda Pemberton, Ms. Jacqueline Woody, Ms. Barbara Dunn, and Ms. Sarah Johnson. Also, Iris and Gary Ball, Dr. Thema Bryant, Rosalyn Taylor O'Neal, Kimberly Dailey, Layla Saad, Peter DiCaprio, Dr. Nancy Spector, Kate Judge, Anita Lin, Dr. Arthur James, Michael Amilcar, Leslie Traub, Howard Ross and the CookRoss constellation.

Also, Kristy Singletary, Michael Freeman, Uzma Malik, Fletcher and Patricia James, Shawna Knipper, Samantha Truman, Sharmalee Butler, Nyki Caldwell and the rest of the Courage to Care team. Thank you to Roger Knisely, Ed Hurley-Wales, Shaun Smith, Kim Brister, Tomya Watt, Peter Levy, Vivien Leung, Carl Books, Zachary Gabriel Green, David Bozeman, Kathryn Stanley, Pedro Suriel, Andrea Procaccino, Nina Guercio, Diane Dalzell, Sydne Clarke, Andrea Sr. George, Gloria Browne Marshall, Tonya Hampton, Cheryl Cofield, Craig Woodson, J. Kim Wright, Elizabeth Woodson, Dr. Kevin Holcomb, Jessica Liu, Dr. Alison Lee, Marlysa Gamblin, Dr. Margaret Larkins-Pettigrew, Dr. Alisa Khan, Howard Stone, Dr. David Kessler, Veronica Moore, Dr. Tina Loarte-Rodriguez, Allison Manswell, Karla Tolen, Mary Ngo, Pax Tandon, Warren Hilton, Meg Kiernan, Enin Rudel, Dr. Uche Blackstock, Katie Litterer, Willie Manzano, Selam Debs, CJ Gross, Sandy Ho, LeeAnn Sims, Angelique Francis, Kristin Pedemonti, Shawn Behnk, Joli Ienuso, Sonia Aranza, Gerald Metcalf, Steve Davis and Leecia Eve.

Thank you to Dr. Kellie Bryant, Douglas Stone, David Kantor, Natalie Holder, Leon Smart, Karen Bouris, Gregory Edwards, Toby Redshaw, George Ewins, Laura E. Gomez, Dr. Kamini Doobay, Jennie Weiner, Minal Bopaiah, Lisa McBride, Dr. Selin Sagalowsky, Rhonda V. Magee, Deep Bisla-Hooper, Rafael Menendez, Dr.

Laura Riley, Dr. Anita Holman, Russ Rogers, Bob and Anne Rothenberg, Candy Young, Michael Sanders, Dr. Courtney Cogburn, Dr. Lena Gould, Dr. Nicole Redvers, Chidiebere Ibe, Karen Fleshman, Jade Connelly-Duggan, Dana Bad Bear, Joseph Marshall III, Rev. Leo S. Thorne, Leilani Sabzalian, Isaiah Myers, Jason Wilson, Bidyut K Bose, Sarah Benis Scheier-Dolberg, Jane Schooley-Wells, Na'im Akbar, Kevin Fong, Dr. Jason Ottley, Dr. Phillip Rowland-Seymour, James C Horton, My Brother Neil Martin, and Maulana Karenga. I also want to thank Dr. Steve Corwin, Brian Pieninck, Richard Goerling, Dr. Laura Forese, Ron Kemp, Ed Seeds, John Lewis, Bryan Lewis, Danny Martin, Camilla Greene, Soul Fire Farms, B Labs, Niroga Institute and Minjon Tholen. Also, thank you to the Othering & Belonging Institute at UC Berkeley, The Royal Bafokeng Nation, The film "Every Body's Work" folx, The film "Nurse Unseen" Folx, New York Presbyterian Hospital, Roswell Comprehensive Cancer Center, Verizon Folx, American Nurses Association Folx, and Six Seconds.

I can't forget my aunts Beverly, Kay, Xiney, Nikki, Deeny, and my uncle Bosko. And thank you to my mother's prayer warriors!

ABOUT THE AUTHOR

Bart Bailey is a highly trained certified executive, business, and leadership coach. He combines 25 years of corporate success with a keen knack for creating safe and brave spaces for meaningful dialogue and has an uncanny ability to ignite change for individuals, teams, and communities.

He has utilized expertise in LEAN thinking to manage functions across a variety of industries including engineering, operations, customer service, accounting, and planning. His commitment to empowering individuals to step fully into their passion and purpose is at the heart of his success. It is important to note Bart is a Six Seconds Certified EQ Practitioner and Certified Psychological Safety practitioner with the Fearless Organization.

Bart is a longstanding JEDI practitioner (Justice, Equity, Diversity, Inclusion) and has led a plethora of race-related workshops, forums, and conferences related to racial equity and liberation for audiences across the globe.

As Chief Operating Officer for Courage to Care consultancy, he teaches both corporations and individuals to improve employee engagement, foster belonging, and minimize othering in workplaces.

Bart serves as a family advisor council member for two healthcare institutions, Morgan Stanley's Children's Hospital of NYC, and Lehigh Valley Reilly Children's Hospital. He's also a long-standing member of the Association for the Study of African American Life and History and a member of Omega Psi Phi Fraternity.

Maternal Grandfather Barto Thompson

www.ingramcontent.com/pod-product-compliance
Lightning Source LLC
Chambersburg PA
CBHW051621120626
46551CB00014B/1892